D0874159

The Lincoln Forum: Abraham Lincoln, Gettysburg and the Civil War

John Y. Simon
Harold Holzer
William D. Pederson

editors

Savas Publishing Company

Manufactured in the United States of America

The Lincoln Forum: Abraham Lincoln, Gettysburg, and the Civil War,
John Y. Simon, Harold Holzer, William D. Pederson, editors

Copyright © 1999
Savas Publishing Company.

Includes bibliographic references and index

Printing Number
10 9 8 7 6 5 4 3 2 1
(First Hardcover Edition)

ISBN 1-882810-37-6
LCC 99-071103

Savas Publishing Company
202 First Street SE, Suite 103A
Mason City, IA 50401
(515) 421-7135 (editorial offices)

Distributed to the trade by
Stackpole Books
5067 Ritter Road
Mechanicsburg, PA 17055
800-732-3669

This book is printed on 50-lb. acid-free paper. It meets or exceeds the guidelines for permanence and durability of the Committee on Production Guidelines for Book Longevity of the Council on Library Resources

To the winners of the Lincoln Forum
Award of Achievement:

Gabor S. Boritt (1996)
Brian Lamb (1997)
John Hope Franklin (1998)

President Abraham Lincoln, November 8, 1863.

The Frank and Virginia Williams Collection

Table of Contents

continued. . .

Table of Contents (continued)

Foreword

Frank J. Williams

IN A MOST MEANINGFUL WAY, this volume represents more than the sum of its parts.

At one level, it brings together a collection of essays that we believe will inform and enlighten the many readers in this country who maintain a burning interest in the life and times of Abraham Lincoln.

But in a larger sense, as Lincoln himself might say, its appearance signals a milestone in the life of this organization. The book is a tangible culmination of several years of intensive work to organize, build, and expand the Lincoln Forum.

In barely three years, thanks to the tremendous support of Lincoln scholars, students, and enthusiasts throughout the nation, the Forum accomplishments include: staging three well-attended, enthusiastically received annual symposia at Gettysburg; establishing a prestigious award of achievement; organizing a memorable battlefield tour and conference at Antietam; launching a regularly published newsletter; building support for the restoration of Lincoln's wartime summer residence at the Soldiers' Home in Washington; branching out as an independent national association; attracting widespread favorable press and television coverage; and most importantly, building a strong, generous, and ever-growing membership base.

Now, thanks to the support of countless old and new friends, this volume presents our first collection of papers from our symposium and related Gettysburg Address anniversary events. We hope that these essays will prove valuable to those who did not hear them and also provide a record for those who attended the forum.

It is also the opening chapter in a publishing program that should continue. As the founders of the Forum pledged in its statement of purpose: "The Forum endeavors to enhance the understanding and preserve the memory of Abraham Lincoln." This volume is offered as a permanent contribution to that important and ongoing effort.

Publication of this project would not have been possible without the help and faith of many people, all of whom have earned the thanks of the entire Lincoln Forum community.

For help and hospitality, the Forum thanks Professor Gabor S. Boritt, Director of the Civil War Institute at Gettysburg College, who has done so much to welcome the Forum to this historic town each year, Tina Grim (now President of the Lincoln Group of Pennsylvania), Linda Marshall, Charles Dittrich, and the entire staff of the Institute for their crucial assistance and warm reception.

Our members again salute our Award of Achievement laureates: Professor Boritt, who stands as tall as Lincoln himself among both scholars and teachers; and Brian Lamb, Chief Executive Officer of C-SPAN, who through his programming and on-air presence nurtures a growing national interest in history.

Thanks are due our Board of Advisors, whose members constitute the most stellar roster of any historical organization anywhere, with a special acknowledgment to the late Don E. Fehrenbacher, whose loss pains the Lincoln community, but whose life enriched it. (Please see our Board of Advisors page for a complete list of members.) My own task as chairman has been made easier and more enjoyable thanks to the hard work and good fellowship of vice chairman Harold Holzer and treasurer Charles D. Platt. Our administrator, Catherine A. Boyers, has brought professionalism and dedication to our organization. And all remain grateful indeed to Robert Maher, who helped conceive and dedicate the Forum, and who helped launch it back in 1995.

The historians whose essays appear on the following pages need no introduction, but to all of them, renewed thanks for appearing as Lincoln Forum speakers and working so diligently to recast their papers into essays for print. Readers are particularly indebted to the Honorable Sandra Day O'Connor, Associate Justice of the Supreme Court. Justice O'Connor delivered a memorable and provocative talk at the November 19, 1996, anniversary of the Gettysburg Address, standing only a few yards from where Lincoln stood to deliver his immortal speech 133 years earlier. These ceremonies are attended by all Lincoln Forum symposium participants at the conclusion of our formal program. Justice O'Connor generously agreed to provide her talk for publication in this book.

Finally, I thank editors John Y. Simon, William D. Pederson, and Harold Holzer for working to produce this volume—valued friends, as well as respected advisors and tireless workers.

As for my own contributions, they could not have been offered, much less completed, without the support of my very best friend, my wife, Virginia, who makes all things possible.

It is no accident that this volume bears the same title we chose for the organization that sponsored and first introduced its contributions: *The Lincoln Forum.* Webster's defines "forum" as a "meeting place for open discussion" and "expression of ideas." That is precisely what our organization strives to provide, both annually at Gettysburg and permanently in print.

Frank J. Williams
Chairman, Lincoln Forum
April 1, 1998

Introduction

William C. Davis

IT IS ONE OF HISTORY'S IRONIES that Abraham Lincoln probably never heard of Gettysburg, Pennsylvania, before July 1, 1863, but then few in the nation had. Moreover, he visited the town only once, then briefly, the following November. Yet he and that otherwise insignificant town are inextricably linked in American memory, and must be for the rest of human history. Remove the battle from the equation and Lincoln would never have set foot there. Remove Lincoln from the aftermath of the battle, and that bloody three-day contest loses its ultimate meaning. The struggle of 130,000 men and what Lincoln said in 130 seconds are forever joined in the minds and hearts of Americans. Their union is that stubborn, and that vital, to our understanding of the Civil War as a whole. On November 19, 1996, six distinguished Americans met at Gettysburg to offer their own wide range of views on the place of Lincoln, the battle, and his unforgettable Address in our history and consciousness. The result is *The Lincoln Forum: Abraham Lincoln, Gettysburg and the Civil War.*

The Honorable Sandra Day O'Connor, Associate Justice of the Supreme Court of the United States, addresses the vital question of civil liberties guaranteed by custom and Constitution. War always places stress on the rights of the individual, and never are these strains more profound than during an internecine conflict. From the outset, the Civil War involved the question of the survival of democracy itself, not so much by the potential loss of the South if the Confederacy should succeed, but from the danger of the erosion of personal liberty that might be required in order for the Union to prevail. One of the many incredible aspects of our conflict is that Lincoln managed to wage a successful internal war with so little violence done to basic American freedoms, and virtually all of the restrictions imposed proved only temporary.

Yet there were and are those who argue that Lincoln, in fact, was all but a dictator, trampling rights flagrantly as he aggrandized himself with power. Richard N. Current, who forty years ago published his *The Lincoln Nobody Knows*, includes the subject of "Lincoln the dictator" as one of those several areas in which, despite more than a century of study, we still do not have definitive answers. Was he a great president, or only a passive man rebounding like a pinball from the events that dictated his course? Did he master his times, or was he mastered by them? And unsaid beneath the veneer of these and other still-vexing questions lies the greater conundrum. If we cannot agree on his role in Emancipation or his impact on war strategy, or even on his storied romance with the unfortunate Ann Rutledge, then how can we possibly hope to define his impact on his era and his place in history? Can we ever hope to disrobe him of myth and make him the Lincoln everybody knows?

Harold Holzer approaches Lincoln and Gettysburg with a background in a realm that itself has exerted much influence on myth, the iconography of Lincoln and the Civil War. There are many legends associated with the president and his Gettysburg Address, myths that still persist in large part because they are so appealing, and none more so than the notion that the people in the audience, the commentators of the time, and even Lincoln himself, believed that the speech failed, that as the president supposedly said, it "won't scour." By examining the *sources* of the several reactions to the speech, Holzer illuminates the fact that even at its moment of utterance, the Gettysburg Address assumed a life of its own, and one bent to the purposes of every faction in the nation at war.

Lincoln tempted chance with more than his own future and the fate of the Union in risking the 1864 election, for by then the issue of freedom for nearly four millions of American blacks was a part of the equation. If he lost the election he did not *necessarily* lose the war, but almost certainly a Democratic successor would have backed away from the Emancipation Proclamation and the Thirteenth Amendment to the Constitution. As Edna Greene Medford ably shows, despite increasing modern attacks on Lincoln's role and intent in emancipation, the current academic argument that the slaves "self-emancipated" themselves is nonsense. Certainly black leaders like the eloquent Frederick Douglass pressed him hard, complaining that he moved too slowly and not far enough. And the great immediate outcome of Emancipation, the arming of tens of thousands of black men to fight for the Union and freedom for all, could not have happened had not blacks, free and slave, been eager to stand toe-to-toe with white Americans. Yet undeniably Lincoln's proclamation came at the time of his choosing, not theirs, and for his own transcendent reasons. And it made a leap that six thousand years of human progress before him had not achieved: he transformed "property" into individuals with elemental rights. Only a radical fringe or the hopelessly deluded could with straight face argue that freedom would have come anyhow when it did without him. Yet without his elemental move, not one step of the long journey that has continued up to this very moment could have been taken. It was quite a gamble, indeed.

In the end, the success of that gamble was inevitably linked with events on the battlefield. Had Gettysburg been a defeat, and more important, if Vicksburg had been a defeat, the Union war effort might not have lasted long enough to receive the approbation of the voters in 1864. John Y. Simon, the editor of the papers of General U. S. Grant, trenchantly examines the relations between Lincoln and Grant and Lincoln and George G. Meade. The former captured Vicksburg in complete success; the latter defeated R. E. Lee at Gettysburg, but then—in Lincoln's eyes—squandered the fruits of victory by letting the Confederate army escape to Virginia. Despite these being the greatest victories of 1863 prior to Lincoln's own visit to Gettysburg, he said nothing about either commander in his remarks, nor did he publicly comment on either general's accomplishment. Simon's conclusions add one more reason for the transcendent appeal and timeless importance of Lincoln's Gettysburg declaration.

Yet undeniably Gettysburg did represent a severe disappointment for Lincoln, not in the repulse of Lee's invasion of Pennsylvania, but in Meade's failure to destroy the dangerously exposed and weakened Rebel army. Frank J. Williams takes a careful look at the president's relations with Meade, alternately cajoling and scolding, as he tried to get the most out of the first good commander he had found for the Army of the Potomac. Too long forgotten is the informational vacuum in which Lincoln sometimes had to form conclusions, and that when finally he received authoritative information of what Meade had done to pursue Lee, the president largely retracted his criticism, a sign of Lincoln's continuing evolution in his role as commander in chief. Yet always there was that echo of disappointment that, when he came to Gettysburg himself, Lincoln could not hail the kind of victory he *needed* as opposed to the victory he got.

But then praise of victory was not his purpose in those two minutes. Lincoln saw greater visions before him. As the authors of these essays in *The Lincoln Forum: Abraham Lincoln, Gettysburg and the Civil War* ably point out, the millions of bullets and the couple of hundred carefully crafted words that both echoed over the hillsides at Gettysburg in 1863 united the efforts of teeming armies and one remarkable man to reshape the transient events of their own time into something with eternal meaning.

Martial Law, John Sartain's 1876 engraving of George Caleb Bingham's painting condemned infamous General Order No. 11, which authorized Union troops to depopulate four Missouri counties in 1863 to quell guerrilla operations. The order created as many as 20,000 refugees. *LC*

The Anniversary of Abraham Lincoln's Gettysburg Address

Sandra Day O'Connor

NO SPEAKER, I AM AFRAID, CAN find words to compete with those spoken here by Abraham Lincoln six score and thirteen years ago (that's 133 years, for those of you without calculators). That goes for me, as well as for Edward Everett, perhaps the greatest orator of the nineteenth century.

Everett was commissioned to be the keynote speaker at the dedication of this cemetery in Gettysburg in 1863. Everett's oration was a two-hour affair, filled with rhetorical flourishes, peppered with allusions to Greek antiquity, and ending with a recitation of every hill and gully where men had fought and fallen at Gettysburg. The speech was considered the masterpiece of Everett's career.

But it was quickly overshadowed when Lincoln rose from his chair and gave, as his secretary modestly described it, a "half dozen words of consecration."[1] Lincoln was, indeed, a poor prophet when he predicted that "[t]he world will little note nor long remember what we say here."

Lincoln's "few appropriate remarks"[2] began this way: "Fourscore and seven years ago our fathers brought forth on this continent, a new nation, conceived in Liberty, and dedicated to the proposition that all men are created equal. Now we are engaged in a great civil war, testing whether that nation or any nation so conceived and so dedicated can long endure."

In the early days of the Civil War, it looked as though the young American nation, "conceived in Liberty," might not "long endure." It faced so many threats. The Southern states had broken away. European powers were poised to intervene, to permanently divide the young nation into Union and Confederacy.

The war posed another sort of danger, as well—a danger less obvious, perhaps, than columns of soldiers marching through the countryside, but one far more insidious to a nation "conceived in Liberty." It was the danger that government at war might use its extraordinary powers to stamp out political opposition. And when President Lincoln suspended the writ of habeas corpus during the Civil War, there was a good chance of that happening.

Because it is an issue of considerable interest to lawyers and judges, I propose to talk today about Lincoln's suspension of habeas corpus. I will make three points. First, I will review a little bit of the history of habeas corpus: where it came from, what it means, and how it came to be viewed, by the beginning of the Civil War, as a principal guarantee of political liberty.

Second, I will talk about what prompted President Lincoln to suspend the writ of habeas corpus in those first few days of the Civil War, when states were seceding left and right, and our capital, Washington, was threatened with invasion. Finally, I will come to the main question: how did the Lincoln administration act once habeas corpus was suspended, and it was free to take people into custody without arrest warrants issued by courts? I think that history shows that President Lincoln did not arrest civilians during the Civil War to repress political dissent, but only to protect the military and security interests of a nation at war.

Background about Habeas Corpus

But first, a bit of background is in order. Those of you who are *not* lawyers may recognize the term "habeas corpus" as a sort of criminal appeal. You may be following the ongoing debate about how to regulate habeas corpus proceedings brought by prisoners, particularly those on death row. Earlier this year, Congress passed a new law making it more difficult for prisoners to challenge their convictions of sentences by invoking the writ of habeas corpus. This new law has prompted quite a bit of activity in the courts, and it remains to be seen exactly what effects that law will have. But history shows that constant change is part and parcel of the remedy of habeas corpus.

We can trace the writ of habeas corpus as far back as the Norman Conquest of England. Back then, William the Conqueror sent royal judges to ride throughout the countryside of his new kingdom dispensing justice. These itinerant judges would, on occasion, order local sheriffs to "have the bodies" of accused criminals brought before their courts. That's where we get the Latin phrase "habeas corpus." It means, literally, "have the body." And we call it a "writ" because these traveling judges would put their orders into a "written" document.

So habeas corpus began as a way of dragging an unwilling suspect into court. But eventually people who were *unlawfully imprisoned*—say, by a corrupt mayor, or even the King—began asking royal judges to bring them out of jail and into court, where their jailers would have to justify why they were in custody. This explains why today, when a prisoner seeks a writ of habeas corpus, he technically names his prison warden as the defendant.

England grew to regard the writ of habeas corpus as a beacon of individual liberty against the gloom of tyrannical government. It was not a "Get Out of Jail Free" card, mind you—but it at least ensured that a prisoner could have his day in court. If you were to ask an Englishman to name the greatest legal documents in English history, right alongside "the Magna Carta" would be the "Habeas Corpus Acts" passed by Parliament in the 1600s guaranteeing this remedy to all English subjects.

When English settlers moved to the New World, they brought with them more than hammers and saws to build new homes, plows and shovels to till new fields. They also brought with them the English common law to build their new legal system. That included habeas corpus. When tensions mounted between the colonies and the Crown, royal governors were known to lock up "troublemakers." And local courts were known to issue writs of habeas corpus to release those troublemakers.

One of the guiding principles of the American Revolution, of course, was that governments should not be able to lock up citizens arbitrarily, or simply because they raised their voices against the government. The Founding Fathers took this concern to heart at the Constitutional Convention. Like their ancestors, they saw the writ of habeas corpus as a bulwark against tyranny. So, to safeguard the writ, our new Constitution provided that "The Privilege of the Writ of Habeas Corpus shall not be suspended, unless when in Cases of Rebellion or Invasion the public Safety may require it."

There was only one brief incident during the early days of the republic when "public Safety" led to suspension of the writ. During the War of 1812, General Andrew Jackson imposed martial law in New Orleans. At one point, he locked up a newspaper editor who had been fiercely critical of the general. When a judge issued a writ of habeas corpus to free the editor, Jackson not only ignored the writ—he arrested the judge, too! Only a few days later, when a peace treaty had been signed and the British fleet sailed away from the coast, did Jackson release both editor and jurist.

This proved to be an isolated incident. After that brief wartime interlude, courts went on issuing the writ as justice demanded.

As time went on, the writ of habeas corpus took on new dimensions. For a time, the writ became a lightning rod for people on both sides of the slavery issue. When runaway slaves were apprehended by slavecatchers in northern states, abolitionist lawyers helped them secure their freedom with writs of habeas corpus from sympathetic courts. Perhaps the most successful lawyer in this regard was Salmon P. Chase, Secretary of the Treasury under Lincoln and later Chief Justice of the Supreme Court. Chase extracted so many slaves from jail that he earned the moniker "Attorney General for Fugitive Slaves."[3]

While abolitionists interposed the writ as a shield to protect freed slaves, some pro-slavery forces tried to use it as a sword. Some northern states let slavemasters use the writ of habeas corpus to force local sheriffs to bring back runaway slaves.[4] But this fight over the soul of habeas corpus—a longstanding instrument of freedom—was interrupted by the Civil War.

The Civil War: Suspension of the Writ

1861 was a difficult time, to say the least. Barely a month after Lincoln's inauguration, Washington was abuzz with rumors that Confederate soldiers, gathering at Harpers Ferry in Virginia, might move against the capital. The Southern states had been seceding, one by one, and it looked as though Maryland—south of the Mason-Dixon line and still a slave state—might be next. Lincoln himself had traveled incognito through Baltimore, at night, to avoid assassination plots on his way to his own inauguration.

In April, in the midst of all this confusion, a trainload full of Union soldiers passed through Baltimore en route to Washington. They were fresh recruits from Massachusetts, outfitted with polished boots and belt buckles, satin-trimmed coats and hats. They had been summoned to man the defensive fortifications around the capital.[5]

These soldiers were greeted not by brass bands and waving flags, but by an angry mob of Southern sympathizers who were spoiling for a fight. The soldiers literally had to fight their way across the town of Baltimore to reach another station, where their train to Washington waited. Four of them did not make it out of town alive. Later that night, local authorities—whose sympathies clearly ran in a southerly direction—burned the bridges and cut the telegraph lines[6] between Baltimore and Washington, claiming that Union soldiers might come back, looking for revenge after the riot. But as one commentator has put it, "Bridge-burning looked like plain treason to the government in Washington, which was now defenseless and cut off from the rest of the North."[7]

Washington had a rebel army to its south and a secession-minded mob to its north. Congress was out of session. Lincoln felt the need to take things into his own hands. Invoking his power as commander in chief, he authorized local military commanders to suspend habeas corpus along the railroad line from Washington to Philadelphia. Essentially, this meant that the army could arrest civilians without getting a warrant from a court or without probable cause to believe a crime had been committed by the person arrested, and without providing the speedy jury trial that the Constitution guarantees in times of peace.

Enter Mr. John Merryman, a member of the Maryland legislature. Merryman had been recruiting local men to march south and join the rebel army. When a Union general found out, he ordered Merryman's arrest and packed him off to Fort McHenry in Baltimore harbor (of Star-Spangled Banner fame) for the rest of the

Supreme Court Justice Roger B. Taney, the author of the Dred Scott decision.
Frank and Virginia Williams Collection

war. Merryman, in turn, applied for a writ of habeas corpus from his local federal circuit judge.

Now, as you may remember, I mentioned earlier that royal judges in medieval England used to "ride circuit," holding court throughout the countryside. Well, the Supreme Court worked much the same way until late in the nineteenth century.[8] Justices of the Supreme Court sat together in Washington only part of the year. During their plentiful spare time, the justices would hop onto their horses and serve as federal circuit judges around the country. When Merryman filed his request with his local circuit judge, he went to none other than Roger Taney, Chief Justice of the U.S. Supreme Court.

The Chief Justice was no friend of the Republican administration, having written the *Dred Scott* decision only four years before. When he received Merryman's petition, Taney ordered the commander of Fort McHenry to bring Merryman to his court in Baltimore.[9] Instead of sending Merryman, the colonel sent back an aid bearing a polite message. The President had authorized the colonel, in this time of war, to suspend the writ of habeas corpus. Merryman would stay at Fort McHenry. This, as you can imagine, incensed the Chief Justice. He wrote a fiery opinion arguing that only Congress had power to suspend habeas corpus. The President could not. The President's job, he said, was merely to see that the laws be faithfully executed.[10]

Lincoln did not publicly respond to Taney's opinion until Congress met a month later, on July 4. Lincoln said that, had he not suspended habeas corpus immediately, Washington itself might now be in Southern hands. That, of course, would have prevented Congress from meeting, let alone from responding to the rebellion. Lincoln then took aim at Taney's claim that the President's job was to sit back and ensure that the laws be faithfully executed, even in the face of Merryman's recruiting soldiers for the Confederate cause. In the Confederacy, fully one-third of the country, the Constitution itself was being ignored. Should Lincoln's hands be tied by the writ of habeas corpus in such a national emergency? He asked:

"[A]re all the laws, *but one*, to go unexecuted, and the government itself go to pieces, lest that one be violated?"[11]

Merryman stayed in jail. Now, Merryman was only one of many people arrested, without benefit of habeas corpus relief, in the early days of the war for providing military aid to the young Confederacy. Lincoln later said that he regretted not arresting even *more* traitors to the Northern cause—particularly the Robert E. Lees who had abandoned the Union army to lead its Southern enemy to victory after victory.[12]

Scholars still debate whether Lincoln had authority to invoke the constitutional provision suspending habeas corpus during the early days of the war. I will not wade into the muddy waters of that debate. I am more interested in talking about what Lincoln *did* after March of 1863—for that is when Congress gave Lincoln legislative authority to suspend the writ. From that point forward, Lincoln faced no constitutional obstacles. He could arrest whomever he chose, without courts interfering with writs of habeas corpus. What did Lincoln do at this point? Did he attempt to stifle political debate, by imprisoning his opponents? In short, did he trample on the civil liberties that the writ of habeas corpus was meant to protect?

A recent historical study, entitled *The Fate of Liberty*, says "no." The author, Mark Neely, combed through the musty boxes of arrest records from the Civil War "to find out who was arrested when the writ of habeas corpus was suspended and why."[13] Neely concludes that, throughout the war, Lincoln was guided by a "steady desire to avoid political abuse under the habeas-corpus policy."[14]

According to the best estimates, about 38,000 civilians were arrested by the military during the Civil War. Who were they? Almost all fell within a few categories: "draft evaders, suspected deserters, defrauders of the government, swindlers of recruits, ex-

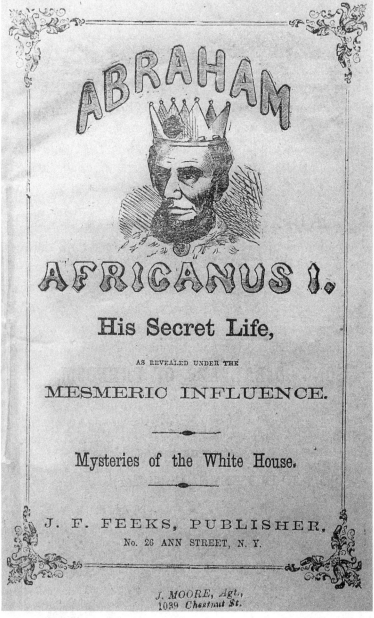

Cover page of *Abraham Africanus I*, an anti-Lincoln tract published for the 1864 election campaign, depicting the president as a self-proclaimed, crowned king. The text included one chapter, "The Fiend," suggesting that Lincoln enjoyed arresting people and conveying them "to the vilest dungeon in America." *Frank and Virginia Williams Collection*

Confederate soldiers, and smugglers."[15] And strikingly, most of these were Confederate citizens, caught behind Northern lines. The numbers show that very few civilians were taken from their homes and arrested. And of those few arrests, only a handful were colored by political considerations.[16]

Indeed, Lincoln issued his most sweeping proclamation suspending habeas corpus not to silence political dissent, but to stop judicial interference in the draft. Early in the war, the patriotic zeal was so strong that volunteers flooded into the army. But as the war dragged on, public enthusiasm ebbed. Eventually, the government was reduced to instituting a draft. Conscription was rather unpopular, to say the least. If any of you remember the burning of draft cards during the Vietnam War, imagine that unrest multiplied several times over in the New York City draft riots in 1863. The problem was especially bad in Pennsylvania. Coal miners attacked men thought to be "in sympathy with the draft."[17] State and federal courts added to the problem. They were churning out writs of habeas corpus, freeing soldiers as soon as they were drafted. Lincoln observed that "[t]he course pursued by certain judges is defeating the draft."[18]

Lincoln's response was to suspend the writ throughout the North in any case that involved military arrest of deserters or draft dodgers. And for good measure, he threw in prisoners of war, spies, and those giving assistance to the enemy[19]—say, by smuggling goods to the Confederate government. But his focus was always on military necessity. Lincoln never tried to suppress political dissent. He understood that a democracy only grows stronger by allowing people to voice their opposition to the government, even in the midst of war. He understood that the strength of the Union lay not only in force of arms, but in the liberties that were guaranteed by the open, and sometimes heated, exchange of ideas. And as one historian has put it, "[t]he opposition press in the North was vibrant, vigorous, and often vicious."[20]

This point is illustrated by the most sensational arrest of the Civil War: the arrest of Clement Vallandigham, a former Democratic congressman from Ohio. Vallandigham was an outspoken Confederate sympathizer, a man who minced no words expressing his contempt for the Lincoln administration. He was one of the "Peace Democrats," or "Copperheads," who originally earned their name from "the poisonous snake that attacks without notice." The Copperheads co-opted the title, wearing the head of the Goddess Liberty cut from copper pennies as lapel pins, to broadcast their opposition to the war.[21] It's a nice irony, I think, to remember whose head appears on the penny today! The Copperheads must be turning in their graves.

In May 1863, Maj. Gen. Ambrose Burnside was in charge of the Department of the Ohio. Burnside, it turned out, is a man better remembered for his long whiskers—or "sideburns"—than for his political acuity. The general announced that anyone within his jurisdiction who was in the "habit of declaring sympathies for the enemy" would be arrested as a traitor.[22]

Vallandigham took Burnside's proclamation as a challenge. At a public rally opening his campaign for Governor of Ohio, Vallandigham gave a vitriolic speech. He denounced the President as "King Lincoln," accused Burnside of being a heavy-handed tyrant, and called for a negotiated peace with the South.[23] Burnside read the speech, arrested Vallandigham, and shipped him off to a jail in Boston.

This, of course, was exactly what Vallandigham wanted. Overnight, he became a martyr for the Copperhead cause. The papers called him "Valiant Val."[24] Democrats triumphantly announced that Lincoln had finally shown his true colors: he was nothing more than a petty tyrant.

Lincoln, for his part, was not pleased by the general's actions. To be sure, he was not *fond* of Vallandigham. The former congressman had been constantly stirring up sentiments against the war, and Lincoln suspected that he was purposely fanning the flames of street violence in opposition to the draft.[25] But Lincoln realized that the arrest was valuable ammunition for his political opponents.

Burnside, ever the zealous soldier, had one more blunder to make. Turning his attention to Illinois, the general decided that the *Chicago Times* was getting too loud in criticizing the war effort. It was time to shut that paper down. So he sent out two companies of infantry, and they stopped the presses.

This was too much. Lincoln had to engage in what today might be called "damage control." Burnside had proclaimed that traitors would be either put on trial or sent "into the lines of their friends."[26] Lincoln decided to take the second option. Early one morning, Union troops escorted a bewildered Vallandigham to the Confederate lines in Tennessee and, there, they set him free.[27] After some confusion, Vallandigham made his way to Charleston, South Carolina. He exchanged some awkward pleasantries with his Confederate hosts, and eventually caught a slow boat to Canada.

The next order of business was to get the *Chicago Times* back in circulation. Lincoln rescinded Burnside's order, called back the troops guarding the presses, and warned his overzealous general not to arrest any more civilians or shut down any more newspapers without express approval from Washington.[28]

Although Lincoln undid most of the damage, he still wanted to make a point. He explained to a group of New York Democrats that he would not allow civilians to be arrested merely for "damaging the political prospects of the administration or the personal interests of the commanding general."[29] Arrests would be made only to protect national security. Now, national security is always a difficult line to draw, especially during a civil war. But the line had to be drawn somewhere, if the Union was to be preserved. Lincoln asked:

> Must I shoot a simple-minded soldier boy who deserts, while I must not touch a hair of a wiley agitator who induces him to desert? . . . I think that

in such a case, to silence the agitator, and save the boy, is not only constitutional, but withal, a great mercy.[30]

Summary

In sum, the Clement Vallandigham episode is emblematic of
Lincoln's approach to political liberties during the Civil War. The
President was not out to trample on the First Amendment. He was
not out to crush his political opposition. He suspended the writ of
habeas corpus in response to perceived military threats to the
Union. After he, and later Congress, removed that constitutional
safeguard, the Lincoln administration did not use its power self-
ishly or arbitrarily. It arrested *only* those people who actively supported the Confederate war machine—people like Merryman,
who recruited troops to march south. And when people walked the
fine line between political dissent and treason, as Vallandigham
did, Lincoln tried to err on the side of free speech.

Midway through the war, Lincoln predicted that habeas corpus
would quickly be reinstituted after the war was over. He could not
bring himself to believe that Americans would allow the wartime
suspension of habeas corpus to extend into peacetime, he said,
"any more than I am able to believe that a man could contract so
strong an appetite for emetics during temporary illness as to persist in feeding upon them during the remainder of his healthful
life."[31] Lincoln died before he could see the writ of habeas corpus
restored.

In one of his famous debates with Stephen Douglas, Lincoln
spoke about how a society that tolerates slavery corrodes the very
foundations of its own liberty. These words, I think, reveal Lincoln's awareness that he wasn't just battling for territory on a map.
He was battling to preserve a nation "conceived in Liberty." Lincoln asked:

What constitutes the bulwark of our own liberty and independence? It is
not our frowning battlements, our bristling sea coasts, the guns of our war

Lincoln looked cheerful when he posed at Alexander Gardner's photography studio in Washington on November 8, 1863, less than two weeks before journeying to Gettysburg to deliver his most famous speech. By the time he sat for Gardner, Lincoln probably had sketched out at least a rough draft of his remarks for the cemetery dedication. *LC*

steamers, or the strength of our gallant and disciplined army. These are not our reliance against a resumption of tyranny in our fair land. All of them may be turned against our liberties, without making us stronger or weaker for the struggle. Our reliance is in *the love of liberty* which God has planted in our bosoms. Our defense is in the preservation of the spirit which prizes liberty as the heritage of all men, in all lands, everywhere. Destroy this spirit, and you have planted the seeds of despotism around your own doors. Familiarize yourselves with the chains of bondage, and you are preparing your own limbs to wear them. Accustomed to trample on the rights of those around you, you have lost the genius of your own independence, and become the fit subjects of the first cunning tyrant who rises.[32]

So today, let us heed the wisdom of a man who led our nation to a "new birth of freedom." Let us always be, first and foremost, lovers of liberty.

NOTES

1. Carl Sandburg, *Abraham Lincoln: The War Years*, 4 vols. (New York, 1939), vol. 2, p. 469.

2. Ibid., p. 455.

3. Paul Finkelman, *Civil Liberties and Civil War: The Great Emancipator as Civil Libertarian*, 91, MICH. L. REV. 1353, 1354 (1993) (book review).

4. Mark E. Neely, Jr., *The Fate of Liberty: Abraham Lincoln and Civil Liberties* (New York, 1991), p. xv.

5. Ibid., pp. 4-6; David Herbert Donald, *Lincoln* (New York, 1995), pp. 297-99.

6. Donald, *Lincoln*, p. 298.

7. Neely, *Fate of Liberty*, p. 5.

8. Circuit Court of Appeals Act (1891), after *In re Neagle*, 135 U.S. 1 (1890) (federal marshal Neagle shot David Terry to protect Justice Stephen Field).

9. *Ex parte Merryman*, 17 F. Cas. 144, 146 (C.C.D. Md. 1861) (No. 9, 487) (Taney, C.J., in chambers).

10. 17 F. Cas. p. 149.

11. Abraham Lincoln, Message to Congress in Special Session (July 4, 1861), in Roy P. Basler, ed., *Abraham Lincoln: His Speeches and Writings* (Cleveland and New York, 1946), p. 601.

12. Letter to Erastus Corning and Others, June 12, 1863, in *Abraham Lincoln: His Speeches and Writings*, p. 703.

13. Neely, *Fate of Liberty*, p. xvii.

14. Ibid., p. 92.

15. Ibid., pp. 136-37.

16. Ibid.

17. Bruce Catton, *The Army of the Potomac: Glory Road* (Garden City, N.Y., 1952), p. 223.

18. Neely, *Fate of Liberty*, p. 69.

19. Ibid., p. 72.

20. Finkelman, "Civil Liberties and Civil War," p. 1376.

21. Donald, *Lincoln*, p. 417 (snakes); Catton, *Glory Road*, p. 230 (pennies); James M. McPherson, *Battle Cry of Freedom: The Civil War Era* (New York, 1988), p. 494.

22. Donald, *Lincoln*, p. 419.

23. Ibid., pp. 419-20.

24. Neely, *Fate of Liberty*, p. 66.

25. Abraham Lincoln, letter to Matthew Birchard and Others (June 29, 1863), printed in Roy P. Basler, *et al.*, eds., *The Collected Works of Abraham Lincoln*, 9 vols. (New Brunswick, N.J., 1953-1955), vol. 6, p. 304.

26. Catton, *Glory Road*, p. 232.

27. Ibid.

28. Ibid.

29. Letter to Erastus Corning and Others, in *Abraham Lincoln: His Speeches and Writings*, p. 704.

30. Neely, *Fate of Liberty*, p. 68.

31. Letter to Erastus Corning and Others, in *Abraham Lincoln: His Speeches and Writings*, p. 705.

32. Speech at Edwardsville, Illinois, Sept. 11, 1858, in *Abraham Lincoln: His Speeches and Writings*, p. 473.

A. Lincoln

Alonzo Chappel, best known for his Lincoln deathbed painting in 1868, created the model for this portrait engraving three years earlier. It shows Lincoln as the quintessential head of state, clutching the Constitution, treading upon a Confederate secession proclamation, and seeking inspiration from the bust of George Washington. The signature, too, is engraved, not hand-written, a common device on period prints that has incorrectly convinced many modern owners that they possess authentic Lincoln autographs. *LC*

2

He's Still the Lincoln Nobody Knows

Richard N. Current

A BOOK WITH THE TITLE *The Lincoln Nobody Knows* might seem to promise the whole truth, previously hidden, about the man. That was not what I had in mind when I wrote the book back in the 1950s. My aim was, instead, to present several enigmas of his life, several issues that historians and biographers were still disputing. My assumption was that, where competent authorities disagreed, and where the primary sources were confused, contradictory, or nonexistent, we were dealing with a man we did not really know.

Since then, there has been a tremendous increase in the output of what might be called the Lincoln industry. With all this scholarly production, it would seem like a relatively simple matter for someone to combine his own researches with the findings of other specialists and produce a Lincoln biography to end all Lincoln biographies. Well, a book on the Lincoln presidency, by Phillip Shaw Paludan, was awarded the prestigious and munificent Lincoln prize of Gettysburg College last year. And a biography by David Herbert Donald, generally hailed as the best ever, won the same prize this year. But these two books disagree on essential points, and other recent writings also differ with them and with one another. Unresolved issues remain, some of them even more hotly disputed than before. So, despite all the scholarship of the past forty years, it is reasonable to suggest that he's still the Lincoln nobody knows.

In my analysis I will include only Paludan, Donald, and a few other recent authors, among them Gore Vidal. Though Vidal presents his *Lincoln* as a novel, he claims it is also good history, and Donald has given it his endorsement. Regardless of its scholarly merit, or the lack thereof, the Vidal book perhaps deserves consideration because of its tremendous influence in shaping the public's image of Lincoln. The Vidal *Lincoln* has been more widely read than anything else ever written about him, and it has also reached a vast audience as a TV show.

Neither as to writers nor as to issues will I try to be at all comprehensive. I will deal briefly with five of the more controversial questions: (1) Was Herndon right about Lincoln's love life? (2) Was Lincoln effective as commander in chief of the army and the navy? (3) Was he some kind of a dictator? (4) Does he deserve his reputation as the Great Emancipator? And (5) what kind of overall rating does he merit?

Herndon on Lincoln's Private Life

William H. Herndon based his account on his own imagination and on the recollections he gathered from old residents of New Salem. According to Herndon, the great and only love of

Lincoln's life was Ann Rutledge, and his marriage to Mary Todd consigned him to a "domestic hell on earth." Herndon was discredited among scholars after the publication of J. G. Randall's *Lincoln the President* (1945, 1952, 1955) and Ruth Painter Randall's *Mary Lincoln*. The Randalls held that the Ann Rutledge romance was exaggerated beyond belief, that it was unproved in its essentials and disproved in its elaborations, and that Lincoln's home life was pretty much that of a typical American family man.

Recently there has been a revival of Herndon's credibility. One of the more persuasive neo-Herndonians, John Y. Simon, concedes only that Herndon "soared beyond the evidence" at times, as when he said Lincoln never recovered from his grief over Ann's untimely death. "Available evidence," Simon declares, "overwhelmingly indicates that Lincoln so loved Ann that her death plunged him into severe depression." Simon admits, however, that "the full story of Lincoln and Ann Rutledge will never be known."[1]

As for Lincoln and Mary Todd, the neo-Herndonian Michael Burlingame assembles a multitude of quotations from acquaintances of the couple to support Herndon's contention that, for Lincoln, married life was a "burning, scorching hell." This is the same marriage that Ruth Painter Randall calls "an appealing love story," citing a "flock of witnesses" who left testimony of Abraham and Mary's marital happiness. Mary's more recent biographer, Jean H. Baker, also quotes friends who had a positive view, one of whom said the Lincolns "did not lead an unhappy life at all." Baker judges the marriage a "success."[2]

Burlingame agrees with Herndon that the country owes a great deal to Mary, that without her, Lincoln would never have become president. It was unhappiness at home, we are told, that sent him out to achieve success in law and politics. But it is possible that the true relationship of home and career may have been the other way around. In the pursuit of success Lincoln had to neglect his family to a considerable extent. Perhaps his strivings as a public man were more a cause than a result of his difficulties as a husband. Whatever the merit of this speculation, it would seem that one's view of the Lincoln marriage depends largely on which set of witnesses one chooses to believe.

It remains to be seen how the neo-Herndonians—those who put such a high value on Herndon's credibility—will handle one of his most incredible stories, one that he never put into print but recorded late in life. According to this supposed recollection, Lincoln once told him that, as a young man, he had caught syphilis from a prostitute. Vidal presents this story as gospel truth and adds that Lincoln infected Mary with the disease, which he says caused her insanity and the untimely deaths of three of her four sons. It is interesting that Donald, despite his endorsement of Vidal's Lincoln as sound history, steers entirely clear of this subject in his own prize-winning biography. So do Mary Todd Lincoln's biographers and most other writers, including the neo-Herndonians.

The Commander in Chief

Even more than his private life, Lincoln's role as president has been and continues to be fiercely debated. The prevailing view for many years was that, as commander in chief, he was extremely effective—indeed that, despite his lack of training and experience, he proved himself a veritable military genius.

Now David Herbert Donald concedes that Lincoln "had excellent strategic sense, which improved as the war progressed." He early realized, as some of his generals never did, that the enemy's army and not his capital, Richmond, should be the primary objective. When Ulysses S. Grant proposed to advance on several fronts at once, Lincoln allowed him to believe his plan was something quite novel, whereas it was, in fact, an idea Lincoln himself had long since put forth. But Donald, while crediting the president with such insights as these, leaves the impression that, on the whole, he was more a military bungler than a military genius.[3]

Far more negative is the author of a new history of the Civil War, just published this year and given high praise by prominent Civil War historians. According to this author, Jeffrey Rogers Hummel, "apologists have managed to gain" for Lincoln an "utterly astounding and unwarranted reputation as a solid military leader." "Lincoln's military incompetence brought on . . . a whole string of military fiascoes in the east." "One of the reasons Northern generals in the west usually performed so much better is because they were too far away for Lincoln to foul things up."[4]

But other recent writers come to a totally different conclusion. James A Rawley in a brief biography, also published this year, maintains that "biographers in general have not adequately recognized how Lincoln's military leadership contributed to the outcome of the Civil War."[5]

And James M. McPherson, the most authoritative of living Civil War authorities, defends Lincoln's greatness as commander in chief, emphasizing his broad "national strategy" as opposed to the usual narrow conception of "*military* strategy." Military historians have deplored Lincoln's appointment of political generals, McPherson notes, then points out that Lincoln made most of these appointments "for reasons of *national* strategy. Each of the political generals represented an important ethnic, regional, or political constituency in the North. The support of these constituencies for the war effort was crucial." McPherson concludes: "Whatever flaws historians might find in Lincoln's military strategy, it is hard to find fault with his national strategy."[6]

The Dictator

While Donald does not follow Vidal in saying Lincoln had syphilis, he does agree with him that Lincoln had dictatorial tendencies. The charge of dictatorship is an old one, originated by the Confederates and the Copperheads of his own time. It was given renewed currency by the literary critic Edmund Wilson, who read between the lines of the 1838 Springfield Lyceum Address to find Lincoln, not yet twenty-nine, confessing his dictatorial ambition. Actually, the youthful orator was warning against the possible rise of an Alexander, a Caesar, or a Napoleon in the United States, but Edmund Wilson insisted he really had himself in mind.[7]

This theory appealed to psychobiographers, who saw the ambitious Lincoln as a kind of Oedipus, eager to slay the Founding Fathers and make himself the great American hero in their place. Donald does not go that far, but does agree with Edmund Wilson that when Lincoln warned against a possible dictator he was "unconsciously describing himself." As president, he was hardly a friend of civil liberties, according to Donald. Suspending the writ of habeas corpus, he authorized arbitrary arrests on a large scale. The administration employed the new conscription law not merely to raise troops but to suppress dissent, Donald argues.[8]

Paludan, though much more pro-Lincoln, agrees with Donald at least in part. "Certainly Lincoln extended presidential power beyond any limits seen before his time," Paludan writes. "If one compares Lincoln's use of power with executive actions before 1861, popular and even scholarly use of a word such as 'dictatorship' makes limited sense." Other writers favorable to Lincoln have used the expression "constitutional dictatorship."[9]

Mark Neely, Jr., in a Pulitzer-Prize-winning work, argues that Lincoln's infringements on civil liberties have been grossly exaggerated. During the first year of the war, he shows, less than 20 percent of the people arrested were residents of the free states; the great majority lived in Virginia and the slave states of the border. Most of these people were arrested, not for "holding the wrong political ideas," but for such activities as "murdering pickets, bushwhacking, burning bridges, and raising money and men for the Confederate Army." Neely goes on to say: "The likelihood . . . is that the percentage of serious crimes rose after 1862 as the Union conquered more and more Southern territory." That is, "the population of persons arrested got guiltier and guiltier (of being genuinely disloyal) as the war progressed."[10]

Neely and others remind us that Lincoln interfered much less with popular freedoms than did later wartime presidents. McPherson points out that "compared with the harassment and imprisonment of dissidents during World War I or the internment of Japanese-Americans in World War II, the Lincoln administration's violation of civil liberties during the much greater crisis of the Civil War seems quite mild indeed." Hummel calls this "the 'Not as bad as Hitler-Stalin-Mao' school of historical evaluation." But the defenders of Lincoln are comparing him with Woodrow Wilson and Franklin D. Roosevelt, not with Hitler, Stalin, or Mao. I wonder what well-known figures Hummel would consider it appropriate to compare a wartime president with. Dr. Schweitzer? Mother Theresa?[11]

As a result of the Hummel kind of scholarship and, to a much greater extent, the Gore Vidal and William Safire kind of literature, the prevailing popular image of Lincoln today is hardly that of a democratic hero. It is that of a power-hungry president who, to gain his ends, did not hesitate to disregard the Constitution and trample on the rights of ordinary citizens. But other scholars, among them the constitutional historian Herman Belz, maintain that Lincoln always faced real limitations on the exercise of presidential power—"the restraints of congressional initiative and reaction, political party competition, and the correcting pressures of public opinion"—in addition to his own conception of constitutional limits and his constant care to seek "constitutional justification" for whatever he did. This accountability marks the "essential difference between dictatorship and constitutional government," Belz argues, and where it exists, even "the idea of constitutional dictatorship becomes meaningless."[12]

The Great Emancipator

Lincoln's fame as a liberator has declined in recent years, especially among African American historians, who look upon him as a white supremacist and upon the slaves as their own emancipators. There is no question that Lincoln detested slavery or that he issued the Emancipation Proclamation and helped persuade Congress to pass the Thirteenth Amendment. The questions have to do with the depth of his commitment to freedom and equality.

Donald focuses on the February 1865 Hampton Roads conference, at which Lincoln talked with Alexander H. Stephens and other Confederates about the possibilities of peace. According to Stephens's account of the meeting, Lincoln said he thought the Emancipation Proclamation, being a "war measure," would be "inoperative" after the war was over. As for the Thirteenth Amendment, again according to Stephens, Lincoln suggested that the Southern states, if they would quit the war and resume their position in the Union, could delay or defeat ratification. On the basis of this and other evidence, Donald suggests that possibly Lincoln "had now changed his mind about eradicating slavery." Or possibly "Lincoln's remarks stemmed from his realization that slavery was already dead," and his "purpose was to undermine the Jefferson Davis administration" by means of a "campaign of misinformation."[13]

Curiously, Paludan does not so much as mention the Hampton Roads conference in his prize-winning book on the Lincoln presidency. But he describes at length the process of reconstruction under Lincoln's plan in Louisiana. He draws from this essentially the same conclusion as LaWanda Cox has drawn. "The Louisiana story," Cox writes, ". . . confirms that [the] president and radicals of his party shared an identity of purpose . . . in seeking basic rights, citizenship, and political participation for former slaves." Here Paludan joins that school of historians who see Lincoln as at heart a Radical Republican, one who, if he had lived, would have led the way to Radical Reconstruction, with not only emancipation but also civil rights and the suffrage for African Americans.[14]

Donald disagrees completely with that view. He notes that the Constitution of Louisiana, as reorganized under the Lincoln plan, did not give the ballot to blacks. It is "improbable," Donald adds, that Lincoln was about to make "any announcement that African-Americans must have full political and economic equality." "He believed that the more intelligent blacks, especially those who served in the army, were entitled to the suffrage," Donald concedes. "Hence he encouraged the education of the freedmen. . . . But beyond this he was not prepared to go."[15]

Overall Rating

The anti-Lincoln tradition, an old one, is still thriving. His denigrators do not hide their contempt for his admirers. "Unfortunately, too much of the writing about the sixteenth President is caught up in the cult of Lincoln idolatry," says Hummel, the author of the Civil War history published just this year. "The perfect remedy is Gore Vidal, *Lincoln: A Novel* . . . which despite being fictional . . . displays a command of the American past that should do any professional historian proud." One of those professional historians has written that Vidal has a "sure instinct for the dubious, the meretricious, and the preposterous in whatever has been published about Lincoln and his times."[16]

Though Donald has endorsed Vidal's *Lincoln*, he does not go nearly as far as Vidal in running Lincoln down, but he admits that his own biography is "a bit more grainy than most." Donald gives the impression that, throughout the war, the president followed rather than led the people. He emphasizes what he calls Lincoln's "essential passivity," his "reluctance to take the initiative," his waiting "to respond to the actions of others." Indeed, Donald sets the theme of his book by quoting Lincoln's statement: "I claim not

The Mower, an anti-Copperhead 1863 print by Dominique Fabronius, contrasted the brutality of the slave system (right background) with the opportunities of free labor (left). In the center, a determined farmer clears away deadly copperhead snakes, representing anti-Union treachery, from an open field. There could be little doubt that the strong, bearded figure was intended to portray, or at least resemble, President Abraham Lincoln—by then a strong symbol of the Union itself. *LC*

to have controlled events, but confess plainly that events have controlled me."[17]

Other historians have taken a different view of that statement of Lincoln's. "'Events have controlled me,' Lincoln said, but what he did most effectively was to define those events and to shape the public opinion that, he noted, was 'everything in this country.'" That appraisal comes from Paludan, and the following is from McPherson, who refers to the Civil War as the Second American Revolution: ". . . in conceding that the war rather than he had shaped the thrust and direction of the revolution, Lincoln was perhaps too modest. For it was his own superb leadership, strategy, and sense of timing as president, commander in chief, and head of the Republican party that determined the pace of the revolution and ensured its success. With a less able man as president, the North might have lost the war. . . ."[18]

Let me conclude by repeating that, where the evidence is lacking or confusing, and where experts disagree, we are dealing with a Lincoln nobody really knows. Nevertheless, I think I know—in fact I know I know—the correct answer to each of the questions I have raised. The only trouble is that, whichever side I pick, I face the tremendous weight of authority on the other side. This does not deter me from making up my mind, and it should not deter you from making up yours. Just as long as you agree with me!

NOTES

1. John Y. Simon, "Abraham Lincoln and Ann Rutledge," *Journal of the Abraham Lincoln Association* (1990) vol. 11, pp. 32-33.

2. Michael Burlingame, *The Inner World of Abraham Lincoln* (Urbana, 1994), pp. 268-69, 326, 358-59; Ruth Painter Randall, *Mary Lincoln: Biography of a Marriage* (Boston, 1953), *passim*; Jean H. Baker, *Mary Todd Lincoln: A Biography* (New York, 1987), pp. 132, 228.

3. David Herbert Donald, *Lincoln* (New York, 1995), p. 439.

4. Jeffrey Rogers Hummel, *Emancipating Slaves, Enslaving Free Men: A History of the American Civil War* (Chicago and La Salle, Ill., 1996), pp. 174, 198, 286.

5. James A. Rawley, *Abraham Lincoln and a Nation Worth Fighting For* (Wheeling, Ill., 1996), p. 229.

6. James M. McPherson, *Abraham Lincoln and the Second American Revolution* (New York, 1990), pp. 71, 91.

7. Edmund Wilson, *Patriotic Gore: Studies in the Literature of the American Civil War* (New York, 1962), pp. 106-8, 129-30.

8. Donald, *Lincoln*, pp. 81, 380-81.

9. Phillip Shaw Paludan, *The Presidency of Abraham Lincoln* (Lawrence, Kan., 1994), p. 316.

10. Mark E. Neely, Jr., *The Fate of Liberty: Abraham Lincoln and Civil Liberties* (New York, 1991), *passim*. These quotations are from Neely, "The Lincoln Administration and Arbitrary Arrests: A Reconsideration," *Papers of the Abraham Lincoln Association* 5 (1983), pp. 15, 18.

11. McPherson, *Second American Revolution*, p. 61; Hummel, *Emancipating Slaves*, pp. 267-68, 285.

12. Herman Belz, *Lincoln and the Constitution: The Dictatorship Question Reconsidered* (Fort Wayne, Ind., 1984), pp. 10-11. William Safire, *Freedom* (Garden City, N.Y., 1987), pp. 921, 971, asserts that the aim of preserving the Union at practically any cost "forced Lincoln to tramp all over civil liberty" and resulted in his "treating every dissenter as a traitor." Donald, *Lincoln*, p. 656, states that he "found especially useful William Safire's *Freedom*."

13. Donald, *Lincoln*, pp. 558-60. For the "eclipse of the image of the Great Emancipator," see Merrill D. Peterson, *Lincoln in American Memory* (New York, 1994), pp. 383-84.

14. Paludan, *Presidency*, pp. 279, 308-9. Paludan, p. 351, acknowledges: "On Louisiana, I follow Lawanda [LaWanda] Cox" and other likeminded historians. For the quotation, see Cox, *Lincoln and Black Freedom: A Study in Presidential Leadership* (Columbia, 1981), p. 142.

15. Donald, *Lincoln*, pp. 582-85.

16. Hummel, *Emancipating Slaves*, pp. 125-26. For the quotation of the unnamed professional historian, see Richard N. Current, "Gore Vidal's Lincoln," *Journal of American History* 75 (Dec. 1988), pp. 1044-45.

17. Donald, *Lincoln*, pp. 9, 14-15.

18. Paludan, *Presidency*, p. xvi; McPherson, *Second American Revolution*, p. 42.

One of the few popular prints to show Lincoln delivering his Gettysburg Address, this image was issued by the Sherwood Company of Chicago in 1905. It depicted an enraptured audience, variously applauding and weeping, and Lincoln speaking without notes, looking almost divinely inspired. *LC*

3

Lincoln's "Flat Failure":
The Gettysburg Myth Revisited

Harold Holzer

SOME SIX SCORE AND THIRTEEN years ago, Abraham Lincoln brought forth at Gettysburg a speech universally remembered as one of the greatest ever written, a gem not only of American political oratory, but of American literature.

Tributes have been devoted to it, re-creations staged of it, and books written about it. It is surely fair to say that no other American speech has ever inspired so much writing and so many more speeches. This paper is the latest, but it certainly won't be the last.

Perhaps what makes the speech especially appealing to modern Americans are the handicaps Lincoln faced in delivering it: a late invitation to appear; a rude reminder that he should deliver no more than "a few appropriate remarks;" the distraction of a sick child at home; an unenviable spot on the program that day—following a stem-winder by the greatest orator of the era—and Lincoln's deep aversion to public speechmaking of any kind once he became president. We have come to love the Gettysburg Address, in part, because, in spite of all these obstacles, Lincoln somehow composed a masterpiece.[1]

We also love it because, as Lincoln described it, it was "short, short, short"—decidedly not in the tradition of our current chief executive, whose recent, stem-winder State of the Union addresses have tested the endurance of increasingly impatient American audiences.[2]

But we love the Gettysburg Address, too, because we sense that Lincoln wrote it in a burst of passion and genius. And perhaps some Americans learned to love it because they still believe that Lincoln summoned the divine inspiration to write it on a railroad train en route to Gettysburg, at the last possible minute.

We love it because we have heard that the press hated it, and everybody in late-20th-century America seems to hate the press. And maybe, most of all, we love it because we have learned that Lincoln himself thought it was a failure. In fact, we have been taught that most of Lincoln's contemporaries failed to appreciate it, too, just as they failed to appreciate Lincoln himself until he was gone. It only makes us love the Gettysburg Address the more.

If it is true that all or any of these myths have inspired our affection for Abraham Lincoln's greatest speech, then we may well love the Gettysburg Address for the wrong reasons.

The fact is, the reputation of no other speech in all American history has ever been so warped by misconception and myth. True enough, Lincoln was invited late, he was told to keep it brief, he did have an unenviable spot on the program, and he did have a sick child at home whose suffering surely reminded his worried parents of the illness that had taken the life of another son only a year-and-a-half before. But much of the rest of the legend that makes the Gettysburg Address so appealing was conceived in liberties with the truth and dedicated to the proposition that you can fool most of the people most of the time.[3] Take the myth of its creation on board the train from Washington. The legend originated with newspaperman Ben: Perley Poore, who contended that: the address was "written in the car on the way from Washington to the battlefield, upon a piece of pasteboard held on his knee."[4] Another passenger contended that Lincoln finished the entire manuscript by the time he reached Baltimore. Even more impressive was the claim by a corporal traveling with the president, that not until their train reached Hanover—just 12 miles from Gettysburg—did Lincoln stand up after hours of story-telling and declare: "I must give the matter some thought." But the most absurd recollection of all came from Andrew Carnegie, of all people, then a young executive with the B & O Railroad, who claimed that not only did Lincoln write the Gettysburg Address on the train—but that *he* had personally handed Lincoln the pencil to do the writing.[5]

The fact is, Lincoln had been "giving the matter some thought" since at least November 8, 1863, eleven days before dedication day at Gettysburg. On the 8th, newspaperman Noah Brooks asked the president if he had written his remarks. "Not yet," Lincoln replied—quickly adding: "Not finished anyway." This means that he had already started writing. According to Brooks, Lincoln further explained: "I have written it over, two or three times, and I shall have to give it another lick before I am satisfied."[6]

In the week-and-a-half that followed, Lincoln anguished over Tad Lincoln's health, worked on correspondence, held a cabinet meeting, watched a parade, met with Italian sea captains, and took time to see a play starring—of all people—John Wilkes Booth. Yet by November 17 he was able to tell his attorney general that fully half his address was in final form. Not long afterward, former Secretary of War Simon Cameron got to see a copy, written, he remembered, "with a lead pencil on commercial notepaper." Ward Hill Lamon, the Marshal of the District of Columbia who would travel to the event with the president, claimed that Lincoln read him the entire speech before they left together for Gettysburg on the 18th. But the notoriously self-serving Lamon could not help adding froth to the legend by claiming that the president confided: "It does not suit me, but I have not time for any more." By this time, of course, he had devoted a good deal of time—as well as thought—to his Gettysburg Address.[7]

The idea that Lincoln did not take his Gettysburg opportunity seriously is preposterous. He did not even want to travel to the village on the same day as the ceremony, as originally planned by the War Department, for fear of missing the event, as he put it, "by the slightest accident." It was Lincoln who insisted on starting out for Gettysburg the day before, to make certain that he was rested and prepared for the ceremonies. This was not a man who left things to the last minute.[8]

Besides, anyone who has seen the autograph copy of his February 11, 1861, farewell address to Springfield, truly written on a train, knows how difficult Lincoln found it to take pen in hand on the rocking, rolling railroad cars of the 1860s. He had agreed to write out the farewell remarks he had just given extemporaneously for reporters traveling with him to his inauguration. But midway through the effort, he gave up. The jostling of the cars was transforming his usually precise penmanship into an indecipherable scrawl. Perhaps the effort was making him queasy. So he asked his secretary, John G. Nicolay, to take over the task. The rest of the surviving document is in Nicolay's handwriting. If Lincoln did write anything en route to Gettysburg it has not survived. But chances are he recalled his Springfield experience and did not even try. Lincoln was too careful when it came to writing speeches in advance, too poor an impromptu speaker—and well aware of his shortcomings in that department—to make plausible the idea that he waited until the last minute to write his Gettysburg Address.[9]

The most stubborn of all the Gettysburg myths is the resilient legend that holds that the speech was poorly received when Lincoln delivered it—that, at best, only a few enthusiasts appreciated it, while most eyewitnesses did not. Such conclusions are inherently suspicious. In truth, eyewitnesses to Gettysburg disagreed about almost everything to do with Lincoln's appearance there, even the weather.

One spectator remembered November 19, 1863, as "bright and clear." Yet the *Washington Chronicle* reported rain showers. Some said 15,000 people crowded the town for the event. Others counted 100,000. Some went to their deaths insisting that Lincoln took a tour of the battlefield in the early morning hours on dedication day. Others swore that he stayed inside the Wills House until it was time to mount up for the procession to the ceremony.[10]

People even disagreed about his horse. One visitor gushed that Lincoln looked "like Saul of old" that day as he sat astride "the largest . . . Chestnut horse" in the county. Another testified that he rode "a diminutive pony." And yet another thought the horse was so small that Lincoln's long legs practically dragged along the ground—inspiring one old local farmer to exclaim at the sight of him: "Say Father Abraham, if she goes to run away with yer . . . just stand up and let her go." People on the scene did not even agree on the color of the horse. Surviving recollections state with equal certainty that it was "a white horse," a "chestnut bay," a "brown charger," and a "black steed."[11]

When such wildly diverse recollection becomes the rule—not the exception—how seriously should we take the claims of those who asserted that Lincoln's speech fell on deaf ears at Gettysburg? This is especially so when it comes to the crucial question: did the listeners appreciate the address? True, they had just heard a two-hour-long speech from the principal orator of the day, Edward

Everett. Drained and likely exhausted, they may not have been ready to focus on another major speech. Then again, they were about to see and hear the President of the United States, some for the first and only time.

Did Lincoln's speaking style prevent the audience from appreciating the novelty of his appearance and the beauty of his words? Presidential assistant secretary John Hay remembered that Lincoln spoke "in a firm free way." But a journalist from Cincinnati complained about his "sharp, unmusical, treble voice."[12]

Then there is the issue of whether Lincoln read from a text or spoke from memory. Private secretary Nicolay maintained he "did not read from a manuscript." A student in the audience, on the other hand, remembered that Lincoln kept a "hand on each side of the manuscript" while he spoke, though he "looked at it seldom." And yet another eyewitness recalled that Lincoln "barely took his eyes" off the speech while he read it.[13]

There is the testimony from the Associated Press reporter, Joseph L. Gilbert, who said he was so transfixed by Lincoln's "intense earnestness and depth of feeling" as he spoke that he stopped taking notes just to gaze "up at him." He had to borrow Lincoln's manuscript afterwards to fill in the gaps, inserting several interruptions for "applause" plus "long continued applause" at the conclusion. Did he really remember such outbursts of enthusiasm? Or did he add them charitably to an address that otherwise elicited no reaction at all? Whom do we believe?[14]

Stenographer-correspondents were both imprecise and partisan in the Civil War era. The real Lincoln-Douglas debates, to cite the most famous casualty of their work, are irrevocably lost to us, since all we have left are the Republican-commissioned transcripts that make Lincoln sound perfect and Douglas bombastic; and the Democratic-commissioned transcripts that make Lincoln sound hesitant and Douglas eloquent.

Political stenography had not advanced much toward non-partisanship by 1863. One Chicago shorthand reporter at Gettysburg,

for example, heard Lincoln say "our poor *attempts* to add or de-
tract," not "our poor *power*" [emphasis added]. And three New
York papers heard Lincoln dedicate Americans not to "the unfinished work that they have thus far so nobly advanced," but the
"*re*finished work" [emphasis added], as if he *was* a home-remod-
eling contractor. Another stenographer recorded not "we here
highly resolve," but "we here highly imbibe." And one Democratic paper claimed that Lincoln could not even count; he had
started his speech referring not to the events of "four score and
seven years ago," but to "four score and *ten* years ago" [emphasis
added].[15]

There was more than sloppy stenography at work here. There
was highly partisan stenography as well, just as in the days of the
Lincoln-Douglas debates. Thus, to no one's surprise, the *Illinois
State Journal*, the old pro-Lincoln paper from Springfield, reported that "immense applause" had greeted the president at Gettysburg. But a far less sympathetic observer reported "not a word,
not a cheer, not a shout."[16]

Which version of the audience reaction was correct? We may
never know for sure. The truth is buried within the 19th-century
tradition of partisan journalism. The question boils down to the
credibility of the Republican vs. the Democratic party press.

That is why it seems so foolish that biographers have made so
much of the fact that many of the newspapers commenting immediately on the Gettysburg Address failed to realize its greatness.
In fact, it was Lamon who fueled this most stubborn of legends by
insisting "without fear of contradiction, that this famous Gettysburg speech was not regarded . . . by the press . . . as a production
of extraordinary merit, nor was it commented on as such until
after the death of its author."[17]

Perhaps Lamon was thinking of one of the most frequently
quoted criticisms—from the *Chicago Times*: "The cheek of every
American must tingle with shame as he reads the silly flat and
dishwatery remarks of the man who has to be pointed out as the

President of the United States." On the other hand, the rival Chicago newspaper, the *Tribune,* quickly appreciated, and announced, the importance of the speech, countering: "The dedicatory remarks by President Lincoln will live among the annals of the war."[18]

I would suggest that this difference of opinion was totally insignificant, at least as genuine evidence of Lincoln's performance at Gettysburg. Of course, the *Tribune* predicted great things for the Gettysburg Address. It had been a pro-Lincoln paper since at least 1858, when it hired the stenographer who recorded the Republican version of the Lincoln-Douglas debates and filled its pages daily with attacks on Douglas and praise of Lincoln. Why would it not cheer the speech at Gettysburg? It had cheered nearly every speech Lincoln ever made.

And of course the *Chicago Times* hated it. It hated Lincoln! It hated him when he ran against Douglas, charging that "the Republicans have a candidate for the Senate of whose bad rhetoric and horrible jargon they are ashamed." And surely the *Times* had not grown fonder of Lincoln after his army closed the newspaper down in 1863—the same year as the Gettysburg Address—even if it was Lincoln who later countermanded the order. "Is Mr. Lincoln less refined than a savage?" the *Times* taunted in its comment on the address.[19]

Nor is it surprising that the Democratic party newspaper in Harrisburg declared: "We pass over the silly remarks of the President; for the credit of the nation, we are willing that the veil of oblivion shall be dropped over them and that they shall be no more repeated or thought of." Those lines are probably the most frequently quoted by historians seeking to prove that the press, in general, did not appreciate the Gettysburg Address. Seldom is the paper's political affiliation mentioned, only its ambiguous name: the *Patriot and Union.* And almost never are the first few lines of its review quoted, which seem far more revealing of its motives than a disdain for Lincoln's literary style. "The President," it began, "acted without sense and without constraint in a panorama that was gotten up more for the benefit of his party than for the glory of the nation and the honor of the dead." *For the benefit of his party!* There, in a nutshell, is the Harrisburg Democratic party newspaper's grievance with the Gettysburg Address: to the *Patriot and Union* it represented Republican party propaganda.[20]

In fact, the Address elicited a number of prompt, rave reviews at the time it was delivered. They came from Republican papers like the *Providence Journal*, which pointed out: "The hardest thing in the world is to make a five minute's speech. . . . Could the most elaborate, splendid oration be more beautiful, more touching, more inspiring, than those thrilling words?"[21]

It is true that the *London Times* did complain that the ceremony at Gettysburg was "rendered ludicrous by some of the luckless sallies of that poor President Lincoln." But the *London Times* seldom praised Abraham Lincoln. Interestingly, a quote from the same review that several historians have used to illustrate the period press's foolhardy dismissal of the Gettysburg Address—that it was "dull and commonplace"—has long been quoted inaccurately. The paper actually used those words to criticize not Abraham Lincoln's Gettysburg Address, but Edward Everett's.[22]

As for Everett, his own assessment, sent to Lincoln the day after the ceremonies, conceded: "I should be glad if I could flatter myself that I came as near to the central idea of the occasion in two hours, as you did in two minutes." Thus, even if we cling to the ultimate Gettysburg legend—that Lincoln himself thought he missed a golden opportunity on November 19—we can at least be satisfied that he knew better by November 20, the day he received Everett's letter of praise and replied modestly that he was "pleased to know" that what he said "was not entirely a failure."[23]

We probably owe the legend of Lincoln's lack of enthusiasm for his own performance at Gettysburg almost entirely to Ward Hill Lamon, one of the most consistently undependable sources in the annals of Lincoln biography. It was Lamon who claimed that when Lincoln took his seat after the address, he confided sadly: "That speech won't *scour*! It is a flat failure, and the people are disappointed." And it was Lamon who added that when they returned to Washington, Lincoln repeated: "I tell you, Hill, that speech fell on the audience like a wet blanket. I am distressed about it. I ought to have prepared it with more care."[24]

As historians Don E. Fehrenbacher and Virginia Fehrenbacher recently pointed out, however, the original personal notes from which he adapted this recollection show that it was Lamon who claimed the speech fell on the audience like a "wet blanket." Lincoln himself never uttered the statement. Later, Lamon simply put his own words in Lincoln's mouth. In short, we have no authentic, reliable reason to believe that Lincoln ever felt that he failed at Gettysburg.[25]

Of nearly equal importance, even if audience reaction was as disappointing as Lamon claimed, Lincoln knew that he was delivering the Gettysburg Address that day to two audiences: the relatively small crowd at the cemetery, whether it was 15,000 or 100,000; and the millions who would read the text in the press.

For several years Lincoln had perfected the art of delivering state papers and political messages through the newspapers. He made few formal speeches as president. But he made sure that when he greeted special visitors with important remarks, they were quickly printed in the newspapers. Or if he wrote an important letter—like the one to Erastus Corning defending his suspension of the writ of *habeas corpus*—they *too* were published for the benefit of other readers.

The Gettysburg Address would live because Lincoln made certain that it lived: By giving his transcript to the Associated Press; by writing additional copies for souvenir albums and charity auctions; by basking in the knowledge that it would be reprinted worldwide and praised at least in the Republican journals.

From the beginning, the Gettysburg Address would be recognized—and applauded—because the brilliant public relations strategist who made certain his remarks were widely read, was also a consummate literary craftsman who enjoyed his finest hour during his two minutes at Gettysburg.

It is therefore fitting and proper to here highly resolve that Lincoln did indeed triumph at Gettysburg, not just in history, but on the very spot where he summoned all his great powers to reconsecrate a scene of death into an unforgettable metaphor for birth—a new birth of freedom.

NOTES

1. David Wills to Abraham Lincoln, November 2, 1863, Abraham Lincoln Papers, Library of Congress; Harold Holzer, "'Avoid Saying Foolish Things': The Legacy of Lincoln's Impromptu Oratory," in James M. McPherson, ed., *"We Cannot Escape History": Lincoln and the Last Best Hope of Earth* (Urbana, 1995).

2. Noah Brooks, "Personal Reminiscences of Lincoln," *Scribner's Monthly Magazine* 15 (February-March 1878): p. 565.

3. Garry Wills, *Lincoln at Gettysburg: The Words That Remade America* (New York, 1992), p. 26.

4. William E. Barton, *Lincoln at Gettysburg* (New York, 1950), p. 173.

5. Louis A. Warren, *Lincoln's Gettysburg Declaration: "A New Birth of Freedom"* (Fort Wayne, 1964), p. 61.

6. Brooks, "Personal Reminiscences of Lincoln," p. 565.

7. Earl Schenck Miers, ed., *Lincoln Day By Day: A Chronology, 1809-1865*, 3 vols. (Washington, 1960), vol. 3, pp. 218-20; Philip N. Kunhardt, Jr., *A New Birth of Freedom: Lincoln at Gettysburg* (Boston, 1983), pp. 65-66; Don E. Fehrenbacher and Virginia Fehrenbacher, eds., *Recollected Words of Abraham Lincoln* (Stanford, 1996), p. 289.

8. Roy P. Basler, *et al.*, eds., *The Collected Works of Abraham Lincoln*, 9 vols. (New Brunswick, N.J., 1953-55), vol. 7, p. 16.

9. Warren, *Lincoln's Gettysburg Declaration*, p. 61; for a reproduction of the autograph copy in two hands—of Lincoln's farewell address to Springfield, see Stefan Lorant, *Lincoln: A Picture Story of His Life* (New York, 1952), p. 109.

10. Barton, *Lincoln at Gettysburg*, p. 71.

11. Ibid., p. 75; Warren, *Lincoln's Gettysburg Declaration*, pp. 81-83; R. Gerald McMurtry, "Lincoln Rode Horseback in the Gettysburg Procession," *Lincoln Lore*, No. 1425 (November 1956), p. 4.

12. Tyler Dennett, ed., *Lincoln and the Civil War in the Diaries and Letters of John Hay* (New York, 1939), p. 121; Warren, *Lincoln's Gettysburg Declaration*, p. 122; Harold Holzer, "A Few Appropriate Remarks," *American History Illustrated* (November 1988), pp. 20-22.

13. Barton, *Lincoln at Gettysburg*, p. 78; Warren, *Lincoln's Gettysburg Declaration*, pp. 122-23.

14. Kunhardt, *A New Birth of Freedom*, p. 215; the AP text is reprinted in Wills, *Lincoln at Gettysburg*, p. 261.

15. For a fully annotated version of the various, conflicting texts, see Lincoln, *Works*, vol. 7, pp. 19-21; see also *Chicago Times,* November 23, 1863.

16. Kunhardt, *A New Birth of Freedom*, pp. 215-16; Benjamin Barondess, *Three Lincoln Masterpieces* (Charleston, W. Va., 1954), p. 43.

17. Barton, *Lincoln at Gettysburg*, p. 201.

18. Herbert Mitgang, ed., *Lincoln as They Saw Him* (New York, 1956), p. 360; Warren, *Lincoln's Gettysburg Declaration*, p. 145.

19. Harold Holzer, ed., *The Lincoln-Douglas Debates: The First Complete, Unexpurgated Text* (New York, 1993), p. 13; Mitgang, *Lincoln as They Saw Him*, p. 360.

20. Barton, *Lincoln at Gettysburg*, pp. 114-15.

21. Harold Holzer, "'Thrilling Words' or 'Silly Remarks:' What the Press Said About the Gettysburg Address," *Lincoln Herald* 90 (Winter 1988), pp. 144-45.

22. Mitgang, *Lincoln as They Saw Him,* pp. 362-63.

23. Edward Everett to Abraham Lincoln, November 20, 1863, Abraham Lincoln Papers, Library of Congress; Lincoln, *Works*, vol. 7, p. 24.

24. Ward Hill Lamon, *Recollections of Abraham Lincoln, 1847-1865*, Dorothy Lamon Teillard, ed. (2nd ed., Washington, D.C., 1911), pp. 174-75.

25. Fehrenbacher and Fehrenbacher, eds., *Recollected Words of Abraham Lincoln,* p. 289.

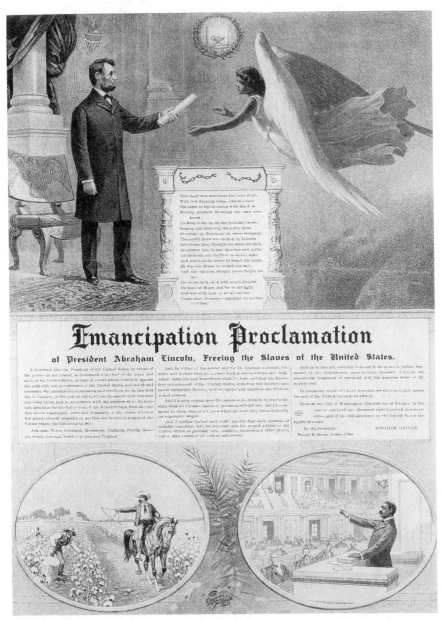

Emancipation Proclamation, published in 1896 by A. B. Daniel, Sr., was designed for African-American homes. The verse on top proposed that the Great Emancipator had been inspired by an angel "looking down on us," viewing "our toils." The print advised African-Americans: "Reverence him, though our skins are dark / Reverence him in our churches and parks." The bottom illustrations contrast the life of slavery under the whip to the opportunity for political equality in the post-Emancipation era. *LC*

4

"Beckoning Them to the Dreamed of Promise of Freedom":
African-Americans and Lincoln's Proclamation of Emancipation

Edna Greene Medford

IN THE NATION'S CAPITAL, a city noted for its majestic monu-
ments, stands a rather modest one that commemorates the man
with whom the freedpeople credited their liberation. Paid for pri-
marily by their small donations, the memorial features a grateful
slave, partly kneeling at the feet of an emancipating president. At
its unveiling in 1876, Frederick Douglass, the black orator and
former slave himself, thought it too suggestive of subservience
and dependency since "it showed the Negro on his knees when a
more manly attitude would have been indicative of freedom."[1] It
is a sentiment shared by those in the African-American commu-

nity today who, like Douglass and his contemporaries, understand the power of symbols for good or ill. Committed to advancing a more historically accurate image of emancipation, they have called for a reassessment of the role of Lincoln and African-Americans themselves in the destruction of slavery. The tendency has been to minimize the image of the president as "great emancipator" and to underscore the efforts of black men and women in their own liberation.[2]

The more one recognizes the centrality of enslaved and free people of color in the process of emancipation, however, the more one becomes aware of the significance of Lincoln and his historic document to the people who were most directly affected by its provisions. Despite its shortcomings (*and there were many*), contemporary African-Americans saw in the Emancipation Proclamation a document with limitless possibilities. To them, it represented the promise not only of freedom and an end to their degradation, but it encouraged the hope for full citizenship and inclusion in the country of their birth as well. Although liberating in theory rather than in reality, people of color saw the proclamation as a watershed in their quest for human dignity and recognition as Americans.

From the commencement of war, African-Americans recognized the significance the conflict could play in their struggle for freedom. Initially hoping to find in the president someone who would embrace the twin causes of Union and liberty, they quickly realized that Lincoln would follow neither a swift nor steady path toward emancipation. They felt compelled to denounce his insistence on preservation of the Union at all costs, especially when his actions seemingly protected the South's rights to its human property. Northern black leaders took Lincoln to task for his rejection of field commanders' acts of liberation, his refusal to back the enlistment of blacks in the army, and his preoccupation with appeasing the border states. In the months before he issued the proclamation, they chided Lincoln from the pulpit and in the press, while appealing to him to hear the cries of the enslaved. When he did move toward freedom, but with the proviso that the slaves be colonized outside of the country, the black leadership intensified its criticism.[3] African-Americans had no desire to increase the burdens of the president in this time of national crisis, but neither did they intend to squander this opportunity for the emancipation of nearly four million that the war afforded. Their agitation, along with that of white abolitionists, produced a climate of sentiment that helped to persuade Lincoln to move against slavery.

When he finally did embrace emancipation in September 1862, in the form of a preliminary proclamation, African-Americans greeted the news with restrained optimism. Members of the black press, clergy, and other prominent leaders of the community jubilantly proclaimed that the end of slavery was near. But during the 100 days between the preliminary proclamation and the actual declaration of freedom, they fought the temptation to consider emancipation a *fait accompli*. In one of his customarily damning editorials in his monthly paper, Douglass gave voice to the apprehensions of the black community. Declaring that there was reason for "both hope and fear," his confidence was tempered by the tone of the preliminary document, whose words, Douglass charged:

> . . . kindled no enthusiasm. They touched neither justice nor mercy. Had there been one expression of sound moral feeling against Slavery, one word of regret and shame that this accursed system had remained so long the disgrace and scandal of the Republic, one word of satisfaction in the hope of burying slavery and the rebellion in one common grave, a thrill of joy would have run round the world, but no such word was said, and no such joy was kindled.[4]

Lincoln eventually moved in the right direction, Douglass argued, but his actions were born of necessity and devoid of immediatism. "Emancipation—is put off—it was made [future] and conditional—not present and absolute."[5]

Throughout the closing months of 1862, blacks remained fearful that Lincoln would bow to the slaveholding interests and withhold the final proclamation scheduled to become effective the first day of the new year. When the South failed to accede to his terms and Lincoln honored the promise of the preliminary document, African-Americans throughout the North reacted to the news with unbridled joy. Black organizations held parades and assembled in mammoth gatherings to listen to prominent abolitionists extol the virtues of the president. At one such rally in New York, the Rev. Henry Highland Garnet (who like many blacks in the North had escaped southern slavery before the war) presided over the massive meeting at the Cooper Institute which had been organized by the "Sons of Freedom." Conceding that African-Americans had "indulged but little faith that the President would redeem his promise of September," an ecstatic Garnet nonetheless told the crowd assembled that Lincoln had always been "the man of our choice and hope."[6] One by one the speakers rose and added their voices to the praises for the man of the hour.

Celebrating Chicagoans were treated to the electrifying presence of Osborne Perry Anderson, the lone black survivor of John Brown's ill-fated raid on the federal arsenal at Harpers Ferry less than four years earlier. Anderson pronounced the proclamation "God's vindicating the principles" of the man who sacrificed his all for the cause of black freedom.[7] Numbering more than 3,000, a similar audience at Tremont Temple in Boston (site of strong abolitionist sentiment), was treated to the oratory of noted black abolitionists such as William C. Nell, Charles Lenox Remond, William Wells Brown, John S. Rock, and the ubiquitous Frederick Douglass.[8] Throughout the free states, African-Americans sent prayers skyward in gratitude to God and to Lincoln.

In the Confederacy enslaved and free blacks, understandably, responded to the proclamation in a subtler fashion. News of the decree reached them through varied channels. Some, using the cover of darkness, listened outside of open windows as their owners read from letters or newspapers that told of Lincoln's actions. The literate few read the words for themselves and later rushed off to share the secret with incredulous comrades in the quarters. In some instances, the slaveholders actually learned of the proclamation from their slaves.[9] However the news arrived, the knowing was enough to alter the relationship between master and slave. Previously "faithful servants" became audacious and went about their work grudgingly, when at all. By the time the Union forces arrived in their vicinity, many enslaved people were more than ready and willing to seize the opportunity for freedom.[10]

In those areas of the South occupied by Union troops, black men and women celebrated "the day of jubilee" in much the same way as did African-Americans in the North. Although not included in the emancipating provisions of the proclamation, enslaved men and women in cities such as Norfolk and New Orleans—where the Union presence had already weakened slavery's hold—welcomed the president's pronouncement as a sure sign of the inevitability of their own freedom.[11] In Norfolk thousands watched and cheered as Union troops and representatives from the black community paraded down the main streets in celebration of Lincoln's decree. Even in the border states, enslaved people recognized the significance the document held for their future liberation. In Kentucky, for instance, news of the preliminary proclamation had convinced African-Americans that their freedom was imminent, despite efforts on the part of local slaveholders to dispel the belief.[12] Elation over the Emancipation Proclamation did not blind African-Americans to Lincoln's other than humane motivations in declaring enslaved people free. Citing the invaluable, albeit coerced, service that blacks rendered the Confederacy, the *Anglo-African* declared the proclamation

simply a war measure . . . an instrument for crushing, hurting, injuring, and crippling the enemy. It is per se no more humanitarian than a hundred pounder cannon. It seeks to deprive the enemy of arms and legs, muscles and sinews, used by them to procure food and raiment and to throw up fortifications.[13]

Lincoln, himself, made no secret of his motivation for issuing the document, having used the phrases "necessary war measure" and "military necessity" in the proclamation itself. From the outset of the war, the enslaved had been used to strengthen the Confederate position. Initially, the government hired them from their owners to build fortifications and perform unskilled labor that freed white soldiers for combat. Later, a slaveholding population—alarmed by the poor treatment their slaves received at the hands of the military, and fearful that their property would escape to the Union lines and freedom at the first opportunity—made every effort to keep their laborers from the front. As a consequence, the Confederacy resorted to impressment, demanding that slaveholders commit a certain portion of their enslaved work force to the cause.[14] Black labor also kept open the South's mines, manufacturing plants, and factories. Those who remained on the plantations continued to grow cotton and other cash crops, as well as food for the army.[15] Lincoln sought to throw the Confederacy into chaos by depriving it of this indispensable labor force.

Other considerations motivated Lincoln's actions in issuing the proclamation as well. In making the emancipation of enslaved people a factor in the war, he hoped to prevent other nations, especially England, from coming to the aid of the Confederacy. Despite having ended slavery in her West Indian possessions more than two decades earlier and having been the country most solicited by abolitionists eager to gather funds for the cause, England's economic ties to the southern states led her to consider recognition of the Confederacy. Lincoln's introduction of emancipation into the equation forced England to choose between a nation of slaveholders and one committed to freedom.[16]

Neither was the Emancipation Proclamation the document that would grant the universal and unconditional freedom that African-Americans desired. In the preliminary proclamation Lincoln had

Courier & Ives provided white America with this exaggerated lithographic interpretation of emancipation, suggesting that Lincoln not only signed the document dooming slavery, but personally broke the chains shackling this representative slave family. The image at least does seem to suggest, in his gesture toward heaven, that Lincoln believed that liberated African Americans owed their thanks to God, not to him—the message he personally brought grateful ex-slaves in Richmond in 1865. *The Lincoln Museum*

expressed his intention to declare freedom only for those in the states or parts thereof still in rebellion. Apparently, military necessity precluded the need to issue a proclamation of emancipation for those enslaved persons under the control of Union forces. The excluded, hence, consisted of persons enslaved in the city of New Orleans as well as several parishes in Louisiana; the 48 Northwestern counties of Virginia that now comprise West Virginia; several counties in eastern Virginia and the cities of Norfolk and Portsmouth; Tennessee; as well as the border states of Missouri, Kentucky, Maryland, and Delaware. In total, some 800,000 enslaved African-Americans were excluded from the provisions of the Emancipation Proclamation.

Despite its shortcomings, however, black men and women expressed minimal criticism of the proclamation of freedom, preferring instead to see beyond its momentary limitations to its future promise. It was, as Osborne Perry Anderson declared, "no matter that the politicians say it was brought about after all other means were tried."[17] Many agreed with Douglass who considered Lincoln's failure to abolish slavery throughout the country a "blunder," but thought the final result would be positive nonetheless. "When Virginia is a free state, Maryland cannot be a slave state," Douglass asserted. "Slavery must stand or fall together. Strike it at either extreme—either on the head or at the heel, and it dies."[18]

The military necessity character of the proclamation disappointed those abolitionists who had pressed Lincoln to oppose slavery on moral grounds. Some African-Americans found irony in the president's focus on military necessity because it suggested that Lincoln needed *black men* to save the Union. His authorization of the enlistment of black troops signaled, they believed, an acceptance of them as men and of his faith in their abilities. There was no small hint of pleasure and sarcasm from the pen of Thomas Hamilton, editor of the *Anglo-African*, who wrote of the prospect of black men riding to the aid of the country:

The skill of our generals [and] the bravery of our soldiers [have] been tried, the strength of our resources has been pushed to the utmost—we have in the field an army as large as that of Xerxes, and on the water, ships in thousands, and yet all these do not prevail, and our tried and trusted ruler calls upon the negro "to come to the rescue!"[19]

Hamilton urged his brethren to heed the call to arms. "What the hour demands of us is action, immediate pressing action!" he thundered. "It is a fight for freedom and we are bound to go in."[20]

Henry Highland Garnet echoed Hamilton's desire to fight for freedom, but he pressed for black men to accept military service as expressions of their patriotism as well. Recounting the rebuff of earlier attempts by African-Americans to fight for the Union, Garnet believed that once the call had come, black men had little choice but to respond to it and "bequeath to future generations an heirloom in which their children and children's children would remember with pride that their fathers were not cowards when the country called them to its defense."[21]

Free men of color had other reasons for entering the conflict as well. Their own lives had been circumscribed by the prejudices and discriminations of a society that judged any man or woman of color—whether enslaved or free—unfit to lay claim to the rights and privileges reserved to white Americans. They now looked to participation in the war to secure those freedoms that had been denied to them for so long. "If freedmen are accepted as soldiers to man the forts in the Mississippi and the Southern coast, why shall not freemen be also accepted?" they argued.

All we wanted was opportunity, and that, blessed be God, has come! Freedom is ours. And its fruit, equality, hangs temptingly on the tree beckoning our own brave arms to rise and clutch it. If we rise in tens of thousands, and say to the President, "here we are, take us!" we will secure to our children and children's children all that our fathers have labored and suffered and bled for![22]

Frederick Douglass also called black men to arms, but ever attuned to the possibility that African-Americans would not receive fair play, he indicated that the willingness of black men to enlist in the military would be shaped by the quality of their treatment. He demanded that the government:

> assure them of protection as soldiers, and give them a fair chance of winning distinction and glory in common with other soldiers. They must not be made the mere hewers of wood and drawers of water for the army. When a man leaves home, family, and security, to risk his limbs and life in the field of battle, for God's sake let him have all the honor which he may achieve, let his color be what it may.[23]

Addressing the fear that black soldiers captured by the Confederacy would be treated as runaway slaves, Douglass insisted that the Union "hold the Confederate Government strictly responsible, as much for a black as for a white soldier. Give us fair play," he promised, "and open here your recruiting offices, and their doors shall be crowded with black recruits to fight the battles of the country. Do your part, my white fellow-countrymen, and we will do ours."[24]

A group of black leaders in Michigan, doubtless encouraged by the proclamation, tied their willingness to serve in the military to an extension of the rights of citizenship. Shortly after Lincoln issued the proclamation, the State Central Committee of Colored Men met to discuss denial to them of the elective franchise and the continued discrimination they faced from "odious and unjust laws on account of color." The committee resolved to petition the Michigan legislature to exclude the word "white" from the state constitution and to abolish all laws and statutes that made references to color. Hinting at a refusal to fight for the Union, the petitioners resolved:

> At such a time as this, when our beloved country is writhing beneath the throes of political devastation, every man, of whatever race or color, who

at all values the endearing name of American citizen, should be called upon and required to do his duty in upholding the General Government, and putting down the most infamous rebellion that ever distracted a country in the history of the world. Whatever may be required of others, should be required of us, and we feel willing and stand ready to obey our country's call, in a summons to arms in her defence, or in any other just capacity in which we might be required. But as residents of the State of Michigan, we cannot feel willing to serve a State while it concedes all that is due to others and denies much, if not the most, that is due to us.[25]

The Emancipation Proclamation alone may not have been enough to embolden these black men to seek the rights of other citizens, but its very existence doubtless helped to steel their resolve to do so. It gave them hope that full inclusion in American society was a dream about to be realized.

African-Americans expected much from Lincoln's proclamation. In addition to it enabling them to acquire freedom and equality, they saw it as the path by which a people debased by slavery would be reconstructed. Black Civil War correspondent Thomas Morris Chester believed that in breaking the shackles of the enslaved, the Emancipation Proclamation

. . . protects the sanctity of the marriage relationship and lays the foundation for domestic purity . . . releases from licentious restraint our cruelly treated women and defends them in the maiden chastity which instincts suggest . . . justifies the natural right of the mother over the disposition of her daughters, and gives to the father the only claim which Almighty God intended should be exercised by man over his son . . . puts an end to blasphemy and the perversion of the scriptures, and inaugurates those higher and holier influences which will prosper all the people and bless the land from the Atlantic to the Pacific . . . ends the days of oppression, cruelty and outrage, founded on complexion, and introduces an era of emancipation, humanity and virtue, founded upon the principles of unerring justice.[26]

Of course, Chester was reading a lot into a conservative, limited document. But he understood that in elevating the enslaved from property to human being, the proclamation would alter the lives of African-Americans in a way that would ensure their dignity and secure for them the right of self-determination.

Recognizing that Lincoln's proclamation was "constructed of paper and ink," and that its success hinged on Union victory, African-Americans resolved to provide the assistance that would secure that victory. Before Lee surrendered the battered remnants of his army at Appomattox Courthouse, more than 180,000 African-Americans had served in defense of Union and liberty; approximately 134,000 from the South and 52,000 from the North. Untold others had aided the cause through their work as laborers for the military; as spies, scouts, nurses, and informants; and as disrupters of the institution of slavery. As the proclamation intended, many enslaved blacks fled to the Union lines and freedom at the first opportunity. By war's end, as many as 500,000 had come under Union control.[27]

But African-Americans had escaped the Confederacy long before the issuing of the proclamation, and congressional action had virtually ensured the freedom of many of those Lincoln sought to liberate. Men more sympathetic to abolition had been moving the country in that direction from the earliest stages of the war. General Benjamin Butler's decision to declare as contrabands-of-war those slaves who made their way to his lines at Virginia's Fortress Monroe had been followed by congressional action that saw passage of laws that first confiscated slaves from masters who permitted them to labor for the Confederacy and later set free all those of disloyal owners who made their way to Union-held territory. In the meantime, enslaved men and women in the District of Columbia acquired their freedom through congressional action, as did those in the territories. While Lincoln supported (even championed) some of these actions, he generally followed a less radical path than did Congress, choosing instead to nudge the border states into taking the lead toward emancipation by encouraging compensation to owners of lost slave property. Yet, in the wake of the Emancipation Proclamation, African-Americans—enslaved and free—credited the president with securing their freedom.

More than any other single measure of the war, the proclamation seized the attention of black people. It may have lacked the depth of feeling, the degree of moral force, that some thought the occasion demanded; yet, the recipients of its declarations recognized the power of its author to honor its promise. The proclamation had been issued by the most powerful man in the nation. For a people accustomed to power and authority vested in a single individual (in slavery, the master) Lincoln's decree was equivalent to divine law. "I never seed Mr. Lincoln, but when they told me 'bout him, I thought he was partly God," former slave Angie Garret would later recall.[28] Even before the war was over and freedom secured, before he received martyr status at the hands of John Wilkes Booth, the slaves venerated him. Lincoln was an icon, but one with whom they could communicate. Their sense of his accessibility is reflected in the letter Marylander Annie Davis sent to him less than a year before the war ended:

> Mr. President It is my Desire to be free. to go to see my people on the eastern shore. my mistress wont let me you will please let me know if we are free. and what i can do. I write to you for advice. please send me word this week. or as soon as possible. . . .[29]

Perhaps less naively, free people of color regarded Lincoln as thoroughly approachable as well. From Buffalo, New York, Hannah Johnson wrote the president expressing her concern about mistreatment of black troops by Confederate officers. After providing him with background, which included a bit of her family history, she implored him to protect men like her son who had served with the 54th Massachusetts at Fort Wagner:

> I have but poor edication. . . . but I know just as well as any what is right between man and man. Now I know it is right that a colored man should go and fight for his country, and so ought to a white man. I know that a

colored man ought to run no greater risques than a white, his pay is no greater his obligation to fight is the same. So why should not our enemies be compelled to treat him the same, Made to do it.[30]

Mrs. Johnson proceeded to instruct the president on the history of race relations in the South and proposed a plan of action to counter the rebel army's attack on the rights of black Union prisoners of war:

Now Mr. Lincoln dont you think you oght to stop this thing and make them do the same by the colored men they have lived in idleness all their lives on stolen labor and made savages of the colored people, but they now are so furious because they are proving themselves to be men, such as have come away and got some edication. It must not be so. You must put the rebels to work in State prisons to making shoes and things, if they sell our colored soldiers, till they let them all go. And give their wounded the same treatment. it would seem cruel, but there [is] no other way, and a just man must do hard things sometimes, that shew him to be a great man . . . Will you see that the colored men fighting now, are fairly treated. You ought to do this, and do it at once, Not let the thing run along meet it quickly and manfully, and stop this, mean cowardly cruelty.[31]

Johnson assured Lincoln that if he did the right thing "When you are dead and in Heaven, in a thousand years that action of yours will make the Angels sing your praises . . ."[32]

These letters reflect the degree of faith people of color had in Lincoln. His image as protector and emancipator had been burned into their consciousness because the proclamation symbolized the attainability of their most fervent desires.

A contemporary observer likened the Emancipation Proclamation to "a pillar of flame, beckoning [enslaved men and women] to the dreamed of promise of freedom! Bidding them leap from chattel-hood to manhood, from slavery to freedom!"[33] Because blacks responded to that beacon, the Union won the war and secured the freedom the proclamation promised. The enslaved needed Lincoln, but the president needed them as well. Union for the nation and liberty for African-Americans resulted from a necessary alliance between the two. As usual, Douglass was right; a more fitting image for the freedmen's memorial to the president would have been one which depicted the slave standing triumphantly beside the equally victorious Lincoln.

NOTES

1. Quoted in Benjamin Quarles, *Frederick Douglass* (New York, 1968), p. 277.

2. On self-emancipation, see Barbara J. Fields, "Who Freed the Slaves?" in Geoffrey C. Ward, Ric Burns, and Ken Burns, *The Civil War: An Illustrated History* (New York, 1990), pp. 178-81.

3. On the African-American response to Lincoln's wartime measures, see Benjamin Quarles, *Lincoln and the Negro* (New York, 1962); James McPherson, *The Negro's Civil War: How American Negroes Felt and Acted during the War for the Union* (Urbana, 1982). See also Edna Greene Medford, "'Something More Than the Mere "Union" to Fight For': African-Americans Respond to Lincoln's Wartime Policies," in *Lincoln and His Contemporaries*, Charles M. Hubbard, ed. (Macon, Ga., 1999).

4. "January First, 1863," *Douglass' Monthly* (January 1863).

5. Ibid.

6. "The Great Emancipation Demonstration," *The Anglo-African* (January 10, 1863). *The Anglo-African*, published in New York throughout most of the war, was the premier newspaper devoted to African-American concerns at the time. In addition to reporting on the progress of the war and on the effort to push the nation toward emancipation, the newspaper featured the observations of the most prominent men in the black community. Its editorials and news coverage were always pro-emancipation and often vehemently opposed Lincoln's wartime policies.

7. "Remarks of O. P. Anderson," *The Anglo-African* (January 10, 1863).

8. William C. Nell was a free born Bostonian who had served at one time as a journalist on the papers of both William Lloyd Garrison and Frederick

Douglass. Before the war, he had gained some degree of fame from publication of *Colored Patriots of the American Revolution*. Charles Lenox Remond, a free born black man from Salem, Massachusetts, was a professional lecturer on the anti-slavery circuit. He joined men like William Wells Brown, who had been born into slavery in Lexington, Kentucky. After making his escape as a young man, Brown became an anti-slavery lecturer and a writer of some note. His book, *The Black Man, His Antecedents, His Genius, and His Achievements,* was published during the Civil War. John S. Rock was a bit of a renaissance man, having engaged at one time or another in the professions of medicine, dentistry, education, and the law. He was one of the most outspoken critics of Lincoln's colonization proposal and the president's handling of the slavery question in the early stages of the war.

9. James Mellon, ed., *Bullwhip Days: The Slaves Remember* (New York, 1990), p. 337; John Blassingame, ed., *Slave Testimony: Two Centuries of Letters, Speeches, Interviews, and Autobiographies* (Baton Rouge, 1977), pp. 616 and 618; James McPherson, *The Negro's Civil War*, p. 65.

10. On the changing relationship between master and slave, see "The Destruction of Slavery, 1861-1865" in Ira Berlin, *et al.*, *Slaves No More: Three Essays on Emancipation and the Civil War* (New York, 1992).

11. John Hope Franklin, *The Emancipation Proclamation* (Garden City, N.Y., 1963), pp. 92-93.

12. Benjamin Quarles, *The Negro in the Civil War* (New York, 1989), p. 165.

13. "The Great Event," *The Anglo-African* (January 3, 1863).

14. For discussion of the use of African-American laborers in the Confederacy, see Bell Wiley, *Southern Negroes: 1861-1865* (New York, 1953); and James Brewer, *The Confederate Negro: Virginia's Craftsmen and Military Laborers, 1861-1865* (Durham, 1969).

15. Ibid. The Tredegar Iron Works in Virginia, for example, employed more than 1,200 enslaved and free blacks during the war. See also Ervin L. Jordan, Jr., *Black Confederates and Afro-Yankees in Civil War Virginia* (Charlottesville, 1995).

16. Quarles, *Lincoln and the Negro*, pp. 136-39; Franklin, *Emancipation Proclamation*.

17. "Remarks of O. P. Anderson," *The Anglo-African* (January 10, 1863).

18. "The Proclamation and a Negro Army, speech delivered at Cooper Institute, New York City, February, 1863," in Philip S. Foner, *The Life and Writings of Frederick Douglass*, 4 vols. (New York, 1950-55), vol. 3, pp. 321-37.

19. "The Great Event," *The Anglo-African* (January 3, 1863).

20. Ibid.

21. "The Great Emancipation Demonstration," *The Anglo-African* (January 10, 1863).

22. "The Present—and Its Duties," *The Anglo-African* (January 17, 1863).

23. Foner, *Life and Writings*, p. 335.

24. Ibid.

25. "Michigan State Convention," *The Anglo-African* (March 7, 1863).

26. "Speech of T. Morris Chester, Esq. of Liberia, In the Cooper Institute, New York, January 20, 1863," in *The Anglo-African* (February 7, 1863).

27. For discussion of the role of African-Americans in the war effort and in the demise of slavery, see Ira Berlin, *Slaves No More*. The issue of numbers escaping to the Union lines is mentioned in McPherson, *The Negro's Civil War*, p. 56.

28. B. A. Botkin, *Lay My Burden Down; A Folk History of Slavery* (Chicago, 1945), p. 240.

29. Quoted in Ira Berlin *et al.*, *Free at Last: A Documentary History of Slavery, Freedom, and the Civil War* (New York, 1992), p. 349.

30. Ibid., p. 450.

31. Ibid., pp. 450-51.

32. Ibid.

33. "The Great Event," *The Anglo-African* (January 3, 1863).

The Preservers of Our Union, an 1865 lithograph by Kimmell & Forster of New York, gave Grant and Lincoln equal iconographic status. The symbolic figure of Columbia places laurel wreaths on both heroes, as veterans and workingmen below wave their hats in salute. Vignetted scenes along the left- and right-hand borders of the image recall the high points of the war, while the discarded field pieces, drum, and anchor at the bottom signal the return of peace.
The Lincoln Museum

5

Lincoln, Grant, and Meade: Vicksburg and Gettysburg in Retrospect

John Y. Simon

BY TEN IN THE MORNING ON the Fourth of July 1863, President Abraham Lincoln believed that reports from the battlefield of Gettysburg warranted an announcement of good news. Accordingly, "He whose will, not ours, should ever be done," ought to "be everywhere remembered and reverenced with profoundest gratitude." In what amounted to a press release, Lincoln proclaimed that the news from the Army of the Potomac "is such as to cover that Army with the highest honor, to promise a great success to the cause of the Union, and to claim the condolence of all for the many gallant fallen."[1]

From Lincoln's perspective, the three days of fighting brought "promise" rather than victory, a theme he repeated later. His belief that the victory was incomplete colored his attitude toward the commander of the army, George G. Meade. Lincoln avoided mentioning Meade in three public statements concerning the battle of Gettysburg.

Reports of the surrender of Vicksburg on July 4 soon followed the news of the repulse of Robert E. Lee's army. On July 7, citizens of Washington assembled to visit the White House to serenade Lincoln. Brigadier General John H. Martindale, military governor of the District of Columbia, most likely arranged for the presence of a band and spread word about the schedule, but this event occurred without detailed planning and coordination. A small crowd gathered before the National Hotel and marched to the White House, gathering numbers along the route. So far as can be known, virtually a spontaneous gathering of well-wishers assembled in front of the White House.

Lincoln then spoke:

> Fellow-citizens: I am very glad indeed to see you to-night, and yet I will not say I thank you for this call, but I do most sincerely thank Almighty God for the occasion on which you have called. How long ago is it?—eighty odd years—since on the Fourth of July for the first time in the history of the world a nation by its representatives, assembled and declared as a self-evident truth that "all men are created equal." That was the birthday of the United States of America.

Lincoln then told the familiar story of how John Adams and Thomas Jefferson had both died on the 50th anniversary of the signing of the Declaration and James Monroe had followed them in death precisely five years later. Finally Lincoln returned to the occasion by remarking that:

on this last Fourth of July just passed, when we have a gigantic Rebellion, at the bottom of which is an effort to overthrow the principle that all men were created equal, we have the surrender of a most powerful position and army on that very day, and not only so, but in a succession of battles in Pennsylvania, near to us, through three days, so rapidly fought that they might be called one great battle on the 1st, 2d and 3d of the month of July; and on the 4th the cohorts of those who opposed the declaration that all men are created equal, "turned tail" and run. Gentlemen, this is a glorious theme, and the occasion for a speech, but I am not prepared to make one worthy of the occasion.[2]

Honest Abe never spoke more honestly. "How long ago is it?—eighty odd years . . ." Almost anyone can now answer that question with "Four score and seven," a phrase familiar to millions of Americans, many of whom do not know the meaning of a score and more unable to identify the event to which it referred. In these rambling remarks, these ill-chosen phrases, lay concealed the ideas and concepts that flowered into eloquence at the dedication of the cemetery at Gettysburg.

Among the myths of the Gettysburg Address is the legend that Lincoln wrote his speech on the train headed for Gettysburg. Two early drafts preserved by his secretaries John Nicolay and John Hay attest to repeated work on these few "appropriate remarks." Both secretaries recognized that Lincoln's finished speech would be so remarkable that they would want to preserve a souvenir of the occasion.

Alongside this myth rests another, that Lincoln's speech was unappreciated both by the audience and by readers of contemporary newspapers. On the contrary, the words instantly reverberated. Democratic partisans immediately attacked the speech because they knew that it had touched a chord. Such words left unchallenged would vindicate Lincoln's administration and his vision of the war. Abuse showered on the Gettysburg Address was a tribute to its strength rather than its weakness.

Only some three months after Lincoln spoke at Gettysburg he was taken by surprise at the opening of a patent office fair when asked to say a few words:

Ladies and gentlemen: I have appeared before you to apologize for not speaking rather than to speak. This committee of yours has practised a little fraud upon me. They did not intimate that I was expected to say anything and I am therefore totally unprepared to speak. And this is taking one at a very great disadvantage, to be called up after the address of the eloquent gentleman to whom we have listened, and the fine emanation of the poet who has just taken his seat. But there is a greater objection. Everything I say, necessarily, in consequence of my position, goes into print. If it is foolish, it does not do me or the nation any good. If I make any mistakes it may do both myself and the nation harm. It is difficult to always say sensible things. I therefore hope that you will accept my sincere thanks for this charitable enterprise in which you are engaged. With the expression of the gratitude of mine, I hope that you will excuse me.[3]

Lincoln found himself at a loss to "say sensible things" despite the fact that the date was Washington's birthday.

Mary Lincoln soon exclaimed: "That was the worst speech I ever listened to in my life. How any man could get up and deliver such remarks to an audience is more than I can understand. I wanted the earth to sink and let me go through."[4] Unfortunately for history but fortunately for the legions of admirers of Mary Lincoln, nobody recorded her reaction to the first draft of the Gettysburg Address, the only fitting title for Lincoln's speech of July 7. Injured in a carriage accident on July 2, Mary probably was still confined to her bed and unable to join her husband on the balcony. On that evening, having said that he was not prepared to make a speech "worthy of the occasion," Lincoln proceeded to a few additional remarks.

I would like to speak in terms of praise due to the many brave officers and soldiers who have fought in the cause of the Union and liberties of the country from the beginning of the war. There are trying occasions, not only in success, but for the want of success. I dislike to mention the name of one single officer lest I might do wrong to those I might forget. Recent events bring up glorious names, and particularly prominent ones, but these I will not mention. Having said this much, I will now take the music.[5]

Especially remarkable about this speech is Lincoln's avoidance of praise for the generals who commanded the armies at Gettysburg and Vicksburg. The crowd that had serenaded the president later visited the war department where Secretary of War Edwin M. Stanton descanted on Grant's victories before noting that the crowd was celebrating twin triumphs. He proclaimed that "the same indomitable energy which has driven the enemy from the banks of the Susquehanna and Mississippi will ere long drive every rebel from the field and every Copperhead to his hole." General in Chief Henry W. Halleck stepped forward to remind the audience that under his command in the West, Grant "had fought fifteen battles and won fifteen victories," a calculation that nobody since has duplicated. Stanton then proposed three cheers for Meade, three for Grant, three for Halleck, and nine for the Union, all rendered enthusiastically. The evening continued with music, five speeches from congressmen, and an excursion to the house of Secretary of State William H. Seward for yet another speech. Before the crowd dispersed, everyone had plenty of opportunity to cheer lustily for Grant, Meade, and even General William S. Rosecrans.[6] Lincoln's omission of mention of victorious generals by name had gone unnoticed.

By the time Lincoln spoke on July 7, he had already indicated his reaction to Meade's generalship after the battle at Gettysburg. Meade had issued congratulatory orders to his command for defeating "an enemy, superior in numbers, and flushed with the pride of a successful invasion." "Our task is not yet accomplished," he continued, and exhorted his troops "to drive from our soil every vestige of the presence of the invader."[7] When he read the order, Lincoln said, he was "a good deal dissatisfied" with the idea of driving Lee's army "from our soil." Furthermore, he had learned that Lee's wounded were crossing the swollen Potomac River on flatboats without any effort by Union troops to prevent their desperate flight. The Army of the Potomac seemed mere observers of Lee's evacuation of Pennsylvania. In Lincoln's opinion, "These things all appear to me to be connected with a purpose to cover Baltimore and Washington, and to get the enemy across the river again without a further collision, and they do not appear connected with a purpose to prevent his crossing and to destroy him. I do fear the former purpose is acted upon and the latter is rejected."[8] Secretary of the Navy Gideon Welles had predicted that if Lee escaped, "Halleck will be satisfied. . . .too many of our officers think it sufficient if the Rebels quit and go off,—that it is unnecessary to capture, disperse, and annihilate them."[9]

On the following day, before the serenade, Lincoln had informed Halleck that he now possessed confirmation of the surrender of Vicksburg. "Now, if General Meade can complete his work, so gloriously prosecuted thus far, by the literal or substantial destruction of Lee's army, the rebellion will be over."[10] Halleck transmitted Lincoln's message verbatim and in other telegrams of the same day added emphasis: "You have given the enemy a stunning blow at Gettysburg. Follow it up and give him another before he can reach the Potomac. . . . Push forward, and fight Lee before he can cross the Potomac. . . . "[11] On the following day, Halleck informed Meade that the president was "urgent and anxious" that the army attack Lee while his army was divided.[12] On the evening before Lee crossed the Potomac, Meade reported that he had intended to attack before learning that five of his six corps commanders were opposed. Lincoln later tried to determine which commander had favored the attack.

Lincoln's apprehensions became reality. Eight days later, with all of Lee's army safely across the Potomac, Lincoln mourned the lost opportunity. "We had them within our grasp. . . . We had only to stretch forth our hands & they were ours. And nothing I could say or do could make the Army move." He had never relied upon

Meade, said Lincoln, after reading the order about driving the invaders "from our soil," which he interpreted as a "dreadful reminiscence of McClellan" after the battle of Antietam. "Will our Generals never get that idea out of their heads? The whole country is our soil."[13]

Lincoln had originally appointed Meade to head the Army of the Potomac after Joseph Hooker's devastating defeat at Chancellorsville. Lee's greatest victory inspired the invasion of Pennsylvania. As federal faith in Hooker's capacity ebbed, Meade began to suspect that he might become commanding general, yet he was surprised while sleeping at 3:00 A.M. on the morning of June 28 by an emissary from Washington with orders to take command of the Army of the Potomac.[14] Lincoln later remarked that he thought the Pennsylvanian would "fight well on his own dunghill,"[15] but Meade received the news encamped in Maryland and shared the national uncertainty about where any great battle might occur. Meade immediately issued orders exhorting his soldiers to spare the country "the devastation and disgrace of a foreign invasion,"[16] words foreshadowing the crucial phrase in his post-battle orders.

In retrospect, Meade possessed admirable qualities for command at Gettysburg. Cautious and unimaginative, best suited for defensive action, Meade held high ground as Lee launched unwise attacks culminating with the disastrous Pickett's charge. When urged to follow the victory with a crushing offensive against Lee's battered army, Meade responded with an inertia which reminded others beside Lincoln of McClellan. Meade's failure to punish Lee before he crossed the Potomac did not end the erosion of Meade's standing with the president before Lincoln spoke at Gettysburg on November 19. At Bristoe Station on October 14 and at Rappahannock Station on November 7, Meade had failed to deliver the crushing blow that his numerical superiority dictated. Further, in both cases, he had pulled back from Lee rather than exhibiting the tenacity necessary to end the war.

Grant visited Gettysburg for the first time in June 1867. Before leaving Washington, he had unsuccessfully attempted to persuade Meade to join his party. Grant was the guest of David Wills, a local lawyer who, as president of the Gettysburg National Soldiers' Cemetery, had invited Lincoln to speak in 1863. For two days Grant toured the battlefield without providing reporters with much military commentary.[17] Wills, however, immediately transcribed a conversation that captured "the substance of what General Grant said, although the words may not be exactly his." Grant told Wills that Meade deserved judgment with "great leniency" because he had so recently assumed command. Nonetheless,

> the army was not properly managed. That the soldiers were not more than one-half engaged in action at any one time. That with proper management the success of Friday afternoon would have been immediately followed up and the result would have been that Lee's army would never have left Gettysburg. This would have been the result if properly managed. It was to a great degree a soldier's battle, each corps and division attacking as to them seemed best.[18]

In the interval between Lincoln's response to the serenade and the ceremony at Gettysburg, Grant had neither fought a major battle nor conducted a major campaign that brought Union victory closer, although he had taken command at Chattanooga where his army smashed Braxton Bragg's Army of Tennessee within one week after the Gettysburg Address. While his victory at Vicksburg ranks as a military masterpiece, its questionable beginnings deserve consideration as well.

In the fall of 1862, Grant began to move against Vicksburg with a thrust through the middle of Mississippi following the line of the aptly-named Mississippi Central Railroad. The railroad ran to the state capital of Jackson where it intersected an east-west line to Vicksburg. Over the campaign hung the shadow of Major General John A. McClernand, Grant's ambitious subordinate ever since his promotion to brigadier general in August 1861, when he took command at Cairo, Illinois, previously commanded by Colonel McClernand. A Democratic politician who had debated Lincoln, then a Whig elector, in 1840, and a veteran of the Mexican War, McClernand represented Lincoln's district in Congress when the Civil War began. Like two other Democratic congressmen from Illinois, McClernand raised a regiment and found himself under Grant's command at his first battle at Belmont in November 1861. Favored in Washington as a well-known Democrat in uniform who could inspire other Democrats to support the war, McClernand had won promotion as Grant's subordinate and outranked every other general in Grant's command.

Declaring that he was "tired of furnishing brains" for Grant's army, in fall 1862 McClernand had gone to Washington to intrigue for greater responsibility and claimed the right to prove his capacity for independent command.[19] He returned with presidential backing for an expedition down the Mississippi River to capture Vicksburg, an expedition predicated upon using regiments of loyal Democrats that McClernand promised to recruit in the Midwest. He had Lincoln's backing but the enmity of Stanton, Halleck, and Grant, all determined to keep military command in professional hands. Stanton specified that McClernand could organize his expedition after raising "a sufficient force not required by the operations of General Grant's command."[20] Just when McClernand would be deemed to have recruited enough men and be entitled to orders sending him South to take control was left to Halleck, who put off that day as long as possible, in the meantime encouraging Grant to make appropriate use of recruits gathered at Memphis. Grant needed no further inducement to move swiftly.

As Grant advanced down the Mississippi Central in November 1862, he planned to have General William Tecumseh Sherman hurry to Memphis to scoop up McClernand's recruits for a coordinated attack upon Vicksburg. Either Sherman would pounce upon a Vicksburg virtually undefended while Grant engaged Confederate forces in northern Mississippi or Grant would drive that enemy back to Vicksburg where it would be pinned between two hostile forces. If Grant could win such a victory before the end of the year, McClernand would remain marooned in Illinois, where he planned to marry the sister of his deceased wife.

In December, all such plans fell apart. Confederate General Earl Van Dorn captured Grant's supply base at Holly Springs while General Nathan Bedford Forrest struck the railroad line farther to the north. Although Grant later recognized that he could have found abundant supplies in Mississippi to continue his advance southward, he thought at the time that he must retire to Memphis. Sherman had already left on his downriver expedition. He attacked the Vicksburg fortifications along the line of Chickasaw Bayou in late December with disastrous consequences. As he pulled back, the honeymooning McClernand caught up with Sherman and assumed command of the army. Together Sherman and McClernand led an attack upon Arkansas Post that bagged a substantial Confederate garrison. In a telegram to Washington, Grant characterized this expedition as a "wild goose chase" before he learned that it was Sherman's idea initially as well as a substantial success.[21]

In late January 1863, Grant arrived at Young's Point on the Mississippi to assume command of the entire army and to assign McClernand to command one of four corps, an arrangement Lincoln had directed. For the past two months, Grant's strategy had yielded no positive results for the Union cause, had cost the army casualties, and had brought no closer the capture of Vicksburg. How much of the strategy had been militarily sound, how much represented an effort to forestall McClernand, remains debatable.

For another three months Grant attempted to reach high ground near Vicksburg through repeated failed initiatives. Not until April did Grant send Admiral David D. Porter's fleet below Vicksburg, march his forces through Louisiana to a point on the river, and finally set foot on Mississippi soil at a point where Vicksburg could be reached by land. On April 30, Grant was at

Bruinsburg, Mississippi, with the vanguard of his army—McClernand's Corps. He had several choices. First, he could have awaited the arrival of additional troops before undertaking offensive movements. Second, he could have sent McClernand southward to fulfill Lincoln's wish that Grant unite with the army of General Nathaniel P. Banks, engaged in a siege of Port Hudson, Louisiana. When Port Hudson fell, the two armies could advance on Vicksburg. Third, Grant's army could advance immediately and directly upon Vicksburg, the rich prize sought for so many months, characterized by Lincoln as worth 50 Richmonds. Finally, Grant could decide, as he did, to turn his back upon Vicksburg and advance to Jackson before turning back to Vicksburg. By so doing, Grant could prevent the relief or reinforcement of Vicksburg by forces hurriedly but belatedly sent for the defense of Mississippi.

President Jefferson Davis had sent General Joseph E. Johnston to take overall command in Mississippi. Johnston arrived in Jackson on the evening of May 13 and immediately telegraphed to Richmond: "I am too late."[22] Grant's forces separated him from the army of Confederate General John C. Pemberton, who had marched east from Vicksburg tardily, and Johnston could not coordinate two Confederate armies which, between them, outnumbered federal forces. The next day, Union forces occupied Jackson as Johnston led his army northward and Pemberton moved southward in search of nonexistent Union supply lines. Johnston, famed for his dilatory fabianism, believed that the only hope for victory lay in uniting the two Confederate armies even if this required abandoning Vicksburg to the federals. Johnston believed that two united Confederate forces could recapture Vicksburg but if one army was trapped into surrender at Vicksburg, then the rebel bastion would be lost forever.

On the other hand, Pemberton believed that he had orders from Richmond to hold Vicksburg at all costs. The son of a Philadelphia Quaker family, who broke his mother's heart by joining the rebel army, Pemberton feared that anything less than an ardent defense of Vicksburg might subject him to criticism as lukewarm in Confederate sympathies. Pemberton's reasons for embracing the Confederate cause remain difficult to understand but apparently hinge on the circumstance of his having married a Virginian. On the whole, Pemberton's decision to cast his lot with the South looks foolish enough to prefigure his future inadequacies in command. His record before he took command at Vicksburg exhibited no military prowess, and he appears to have advanced in rank to lieutenant general without earning promotion. Part of this success may have reflected Confederate satisfaction in capturing the affections of someone without clear reason for embracing the cause. His indecision during the Vicksburg campaign cost the South dearly.[23]

After Grant crossed the river, Pemberton could hardly have helped him more. He retained most of his strength at Vicksburg while Union forces secured their position in Mississippi; he advanced from Vicksburg toward Jackson too late to support Johnston's army; he then returned slowly to Vicksburg incurring heavy losses. As supplies diminished in besieged Vicksburg, Pemberton anticipated relief from Confederate forces that he should not realistically have expected. Although Grant's drive toward Jackson was a breathtaking example of military strategy, he had benefited from the ineptitude of Pemberton as Meade had benefited from the rashness of Lee. Gettysburg and Vicksburg produced either great Union triumphs or Confederate losses, a distinction not merely one of perspective.

McClernand was another major loser in the Vicksburg campaign. After driving Pemberton back within his lines at Vicksburg, Grant had tried to capture the Confederate citadel by direct assault on May 19. Repulsed with significant loss, Grant tried again three days later with similar results. Reports from McClernand that exaggerated the extent of gains by his corps prompted Grant to commit more men to a fruitless assault and exacerbated casualties.

Grant then settled into a siege. Before Vicksburg fell, McClernand issued a proclamation to his men, characteristically claiming for them and for himself disproportionate credit for the success of the campaign thus far. Because the document had not first been submitted to headquarters, Grant employed what might best have been labeled a clerical oversight to remove McClernand from command. McClernand fell three weeks before Vicksburg surrendered. His anguished appeals to Washington received little response amid rejoicing over military victory. If much of the early strategy of the Vicksburg campaign had revolved around efforts to frustrate McClernand's ambitions, Lincoln was unwilling to pursue the matter. Such squabbling among commanders, however, hardly enhanced Lincoln's appreciation of military attitudes. Grant sent his adjutant, General John A. Rawlins, to Washington immediately after the fall of Vicksburg to justify the removal of McClernand to Lincoln and his cabinet.[24] By taking on Grant, McClernand ultimately blighted both his military and his political career by challenging Lincoln's most successful commander. On the other hand, Grant had frustrated Lincoln's clear instructions to retain McClernand in a key military role. Only the dramatic capture of the Confederate Gibraltar compensated for Grant's unwillingness to cooperate in Lincoln's plan to harness Democratic leadership to the Union cause.

Although omitting his name from his speech to the serenaders on July 7, Lincoln wrote Grant an extraordinary private letter six days later:

> I do not remember that you and I ever met personally. I write this now as a grateful acknowledgment for the almost inestimable service you have done the country. I wish to say a word further. When you first reached the vicinity of Vicksburg, I thought you should do, what you finally did—march the troops across the neck, run the batteries with the transports, and thus go below; and I never had any faith, except a general hope that you knew better than I, that the Yazoo Pass expedition, and the like, could succeed. When you got below, and took Port-Gibson, Grand Gulf,

and vicinity, I thought you should go down the river and join Gen. Banks; and when you turned Northward East of the Big Black, I feared it was a mistake. I now wish to make the personal acknowledgment that you were right, and I was wrong.[25]

The letter was sufficiently overwhelming that when Lincoln asked Grant on August 9: "Did you receive a short letter from me, dated the 13th of July?"[26] Grant replied that "Your letter of the 13th of July was also duly received"[27] and wrote nothing more about the matter. Grant feared that he might receive a call to take command in the East.[28]

Through his letter to Grant, Lincoln demonstrated willingness to credit a successful general privately. The day after writing to Grant, Lincoln condemned an unsuccessful general in even greater privacy. In response to a telegram from Halleck stating that "the escape of Lee's army without another battle has created great dissatisfaction in the mind of the President," Meade had asked to be relieved of command.[29] Halleck responded that his telegram "was not intended as a censure, but as a stimulus to an active pursuit."[30] Lincoln decided to explain the matter more fully. After congratulating Meade for his victory at Gettysburg, Lincoln wrote of his "deep distress" that Lee was allowed to retreat without pursuit. "I do not believe you appreciate the magnitude of the misfortune involved in Lee's escape," Lincoln wrote. "He was within your easy grasp, and to have closed upon him would, in connection with our other late successes, have ended the war. As it is, the war will be prolonged indefinitely. . . . Your golden opportunity is gone, and I am distressed immeasureably because of it."[31] Lincoln never signed nor sent this letter. What good would it have done? Ten years later, Lincoln's son Robert began to tell friends that on this day his father had proposed to send a telegram to Meade ordering him to attack before Lee crossed the river. "If you fail, this dispatch will clear you from all responsibility and if you succeed you may destroy it."[32] Although Robert told and retold this anecdote frequently, its authenticity remains questionable.

Unquestionable, however, is Lincoln's deep distress when Lee crossed to safety. "If I had gone up there, I could have whipped them myself,"[33] Lincoln told his son.

Nonetheless, Meade remained inseparable from the victory at Gettysburg. For the cemetery dedication in November, Edward Everett was selected as the orator. President of Harvard, congressman and senator, governor of Massachusetts, minister to Great Britain, secretary of state, candidate for vice president, Everett was also a celebrated orator whose speeches had earned an estimated $100,000 in speaking fees, $58,000 earmarked for the restoration of Mount Vernon. To prepare for his Gettysburg oration, Everett spent three days touring the field. He also digested information furnished by Meade's aide Theodore Lyman and anything else he could locate in both Union and Confederate sources. His oration assumed that the contending armies at Gettysburg contained equal numbers. He compared the battle to that at Waterloo and speculated that if "Meade, like the Duke of Wellington, had had the assistance of a powerful auxiliary army to take up the pursuit, the route of the Rebels would have been as complete as that of Napoleon."[34] Meade, who did not attend the dedication, would have been gratified by Everett's oration. Nor could he possibly have taken offense at the few appropriate remarks offered by President Lincoln, who honored "the brave men, living and dead, who struggled here," especially "those who here gave their lives."

In Lincoln's tributes to the soldiers who fought and fell at Gettysburg the absence of any mention of their commander has generally been overlooked. Perhaps the time has come to pay attention not only to what Lincoln said at Gettysburg but also to what he left unsaid. Lincoln had not forgotten his dismay about Meade's failure to pursue Lee, to complete the victory and possibly to end the war. He did not, however, hold unrealistic views of the importance of generals in waging war. Although he had specific reason to refrain from praising Meade, he did not then or later fill the air with excessive commendations of Grant. Critics have noted an American propensity for undue deference to their deceased statesmen and generals, including a propensity to honor commanders at the expense of their troops. Lincoln's omission of Meade's name at Gettysburg, hardly accidental, contributed to the universal and timeless quality of the Gettysburg Address.

NOTES

1. Roy P. Basler *et al.*, eds., *The Collected Works of Abraham Lincoln*, 9 vols. (New Brunswick, N.J.,1953-55), vol. 6, p. 314.

2. Ibid., vol. 6, pp. 319-20.

3. Sidney Kramer, "Lincoln at the Fair," *Abraham Lincoln Quarterly* (1945) vol. 3, p. 341; Lincoln, *Works*, vol. 7, pp. 197-98.

4. Carl Sandburg and Paul M. Angle, *Mary Lincoln: Wife and Widow* (New York, 1932), pp. 111-12; Kramer, "Lincoln at the Fair," pp. 340-43.

5. Lincoln, *Works*, vol. 6, p. 320.

6. *National Intelligencer*, July 8, 1863; *New York Times*, July 8, 1863; *New York Tribune*, July 8, 1863.

7. General Orders No. 68, July 4, 1863, *The War of the Rebellion: A Compilation of the Official Records of the Union and Confederate Armies*, 128 vols. (Washington, 1880-1901), Series I, vol. 27, pt. 3, p. 519. All references are to Series I.

8. Lincoln to Halleck, July 6, 1863, Lincoln, *Works*, vol. 6, p. 318.

9. July 4, 1863, *Diary of Gideon Welles*, Howard K. Beale, ed., 3 vols. (New York, 1960), vol. 1, p. 358.

10. Lincoln to Halleck, [July 7, 1863], Lincoln, *Works*, vol. 6, p. 319.

11. Halleck to Meade, July 7, 1863, *OR* 27, pt. 1, p. 82; Halleck to Meade, July 7, 1863, ibid., p. 83.

12. Halleck to Meade, July 8, 1863, ibid., p. 84.

13. July 14, 1863, Tyler Dennett, ed., *Lincoln and the Civil War in the Diaries and Letters of John Hay* (New York, 1939), p. 67.

14. Meade to Mrs. Meade, June 29, 1863, in George Meade, *The Life and Letters of George Gordon Meade*, 2 vols. (New York, 1913), vol. 2, pp. 11-12.

15. George C. Gorham, *Life and Public Services of Edwin M. Stanton*, 2 vols. (Boston and New York, 1899), vol. 2, p. 99.

16. General Orders No. 67, June 28, 1863, Meade, *Meade*, vol. 2, p. 5.

17. Grant to David Wills, May 14, 1867, *The Papers of Ulysses S. Grant*, 22 vols. (Carbondale and Edwardsville, 1967-), vol. 17, pp. 145-46; *New York Herald*, June 21, 1867; *Philadelphia Inquirer*, June 21, 24, 1867; *New York Tribune*, June 21, 1867; *New York Times*, June 20-22, 1867.

18. *Philadelphia Press*, May 19, 1893.

19. Adam Badeau, *Military History of Ulysses S. Grant*, 3 vols. (New York, 1868-81), vol. 1, p. 128.

20. *OR* 27, pt. 2, p. 282.

21. Grant to Halleck, January 11, 1863, Grant, *Papers*, vol. 7, p. 209.

22. Craig L. Symonds, *Joseph E. Johnston: A Civil War Biography* (New York, 1992), p. 205.

23. Michael B. Ballard, *Pemberton: A Biography* (Jackson, Miss., 1991).

24. July 31, 1863, Welles, *Diary*, vol. 1, pp. 386-87.

25. Lincoln to Grant, July 13, 1863, Lincoln, *Works*, vol. 6, p. 326.

26. Lincoln to Grant, August 9, 1863, ibid., p. 374.

27. Grant to Lincoln, August 23, 1863, Grant, *Papers*, vol. 9, p. 195.

28. Grant to Dana, August 5, 1863, ibid., pp. 145-47; Grant to Washburne, August 30, 1863, ibid., pp. 217-19; John Russell Young, *Around the World with General Grant*, 2 vols. (New York, 1879), vol. 2, p. 463. See Meade, *Meade*, vol. 2, p. 137.

29. Halleck to Meade, July 14, 1863, 1:00 P.M, *OR* 27, pt. 1, p. 92; Meade to Halleck, July 14, 1863, 2:30 P.M., ibid., p. 93.

30. Halleck to Meade, July 14, 1863, 4:30 P.M., ibid., pp. 93-94.

31. Lincoln to Meade, July 14, 1863, Lincoln, *Works*, vol. 6, pp. 327-28.

32. Gabor Boritt, "'Unfinished Work': Lincoln, Meade, and Gettysburg," in Boritt, ed., *Lincoln's Generals* (New York, 1994), p. 99.

33. July 15, 1863, Hay, *Diary*, p. 67.

34. Louis A. Warren, *Lincoln's Gettysburg Declaration* (Fort Wayne, 1964), p. 200.

Abraham Lincoln is depicted as a puppet master in *Master Abraham Gets a New Toy*, an 1862 engraved cartoon from the *Southern Illustrated News*. The ridiculous figure of the commander-in-chief introduces his latest army commander, "Fighting Joe" Hooker, before a shelf full of discards, including Winfield Scott, Irvin McDowell, John Fremont, John Pope, Nathaniel Banks, Ambrose Burnside, and George McClellan.
Harold Holzer Collection

6

Abraham Lincoln, Puppet Master:
The President and General George Gordon
Meade, an Evolving Commander in Chief

Frank J. Williams

PRESIDENTS, SOLDIERS, AND OFFICERS must act under conditions of changing circumstances. They do not have the luxury of hindsight to know what to do at the moment. Moreover, since both civilian presidents and military leaders are human beings, they have the capacity to develop in their roles or to regress. If one thing is certain about Abraham Lincoln it is that he is the prototype of the maturing political leader. This essay explores another dimension of him—his capacity as the sixteenth president of the United States to act as the commander in chief in his dealings with General George G. Meade after the Federal victory at Gettysburg.

His role as commander in chief is certainly more questionable than his political functions since his military experience was as limited as his formal schooling.

A Military or Political Question?

The essential question to be addressed is whether General Meade missed a golden opportunity to crush General Robert E. Lee's retreating army after the battle of Gettysburg. Military leaders at the time differed in their answer to this question, as did members of the cabinet.[1] Even historians today remain divided. For example, Gabor Boritt finds that the general fell short of the president's reasonable expectations to follow up his Gettysburg victory with a vigorous pursuit of Lee's retreating columns.[2] On the other hand, A. Wilson Greene believes that Meade was "prudent" and his pursuit was vigorous under the circumstances.[3] As on a number of issues involving a multi-dimensional president, Lincoln seemingly took both sides, initially condemning him and then later moderating his view.

Meade's Military Situation: To Chase or to Destroy?

Major General George Meade had been appointed commander of the Army of the Potomac only four days before the battle of Gettysburg.[4]

The battle at Gettysburg had considerably diminished the army's strength and command structure. Total losses were placed at more than 23,000, including corps commander John F. Reynolds and several brigade commanders. Further officer losses down the chain of command numbered 300. Corps commanders Winfield Scott Hancock and Daniel E. Sickles were severely wounded, as was the army's chief of staff, Daniel Butterfield.[5] These losses amounted to a serious reduction in the driving power of the Army of the Potomac. While the Confederate force had

Major General George Gordon Meade
USAMHI

suffered similarly—over 28,000 killed, wounded or captured—it still remained a fighting force.

Despite the hardships and exhaustion, the Army of the Potomac still retained good morale.[6] The exhaustion extended to the army commander who, on July 8th, wrote his wife from his new base in Frederick, Maryland, "From the time I took command till to-day, now over ten days, I have not changed my clothes, have not had a regular night's rest, and many nights not a wink of sleep, and for several days did not even wash my face and hands, no regular food, and all the time in a great state of mental anxiety."[7]

Lee remained in position all during the 4th of July to see if Meade would counterattack. He sent all of his Confederate ambulances and wagons under Brigadier General John Imboden through Cashtown Pass to Williamsport, Maryland, on the Potomac River, where he hoped to recross into Virginia. Meade likewise held to his positions in the event Lee were to try another assault. At sunset on the 4th, Lee sent his infantry toward the mountains with A. P. Hill in the lead followed by James Longstreet and Richard Ewell. They would take the shortest route to Williamsport by the Fairfield Road and Hagerstown, Maryland. A heavy rain on the 4th added to the difficulties of withdrawal and Meade's ability to confirm it.

After receiving reports from signal officers of long Confederate columns heading westward, Meade assembled his generals for counsel. Keeping in mind his overriding instructions from General in Chief Henry W. Halleck to protect Washington and Baltimore, most advisors recommended staying at Gettysburg rather than pursuing Lee towards Williamsport.[8] Meade nonetheless adopted a plan of a cavalry pursuit. Infantry would follow east of the mountains in an effort to intercept Lee before he crossed the Potomac.[9]

On July 8 Meade concentrated his army in Middletown and for the next four days carefully maneuvered closer to Lee's defenses. Meade reported to Halleck that the Confederates had entrenched themselves in a line from Falling Waters northeast to near Hagerstown. Halleck advised Meade to "postpone a general battle till you can concentrate all your forces and get up your reserves and reinforcements." He warned against "partial combats" and promised reinforcements.[10] All in all there were about 80,000 men armed and equipped compared with Lee's 50,000.[11]

Lee had anticipated an attack and had prepared a defensive perimeter with his right on the Potomac. He took advantage of every ridge and hill. His line ran northward and curved west to the wooded banks of a creek occupied by Ewell on the left for a total of seven and a half miles. Earthworks cut across all roads in the area and effective cover was afforded by artillery on the heights. While the Federals constructed their own works, Meade had made bolder plans: "It is my intention to attack . . . to-morrow," he informed Halleck at 4:30 P.M. on July 12.[12] He added the qualifying clause, "unless something intervenes to prevent it," suggesting his insecurity. Meade assembled his commanders that evening. Only two endorsed his offensive plans—arguing that they did not have enough knowledge about Lee's strength and position. Meade postponed the assault pending a reconnaissance on the 13th.[13]

He has been much criticized for deferring to his generals and even abrogating his responsibility as commanding general. When Meade reported the postponement to Halleck, the general in chief advised him to follow his own judgment. Moreover, he admonished him not to call councils of war since it is "proverbial that councils of war never fight."[14] During the following day, weather hampered Meade's observation but he announced nonetheless that, "We shall have a great battle tomorrow."[15] Meade ordered four divisions to advance at 7:00 A.M. anticipating that such a large reconnaissance would lead to a general engagement.

Unknown to him, Lee had decided to retreat after making a bridge at Falling Waters and after the Potomac had dropped enough to enable Ewell to ford at Williamsport. By the morning of July 14, most of Lee's men had crossed to Virginia. As an inadequate consolation, Meade could claim some success against Lee's rear guard under the command of General Henry Heth at Falling Waters, where John Buford's and Judson Kilpatrick's cavalry captured over 500 men, two guns, two battle flags, and small arms. Confederate General Pettigrew was also mortally wounded in the Union attack.[16]

Lincoln's Military and Political Situation

Misunderstanding of Meade's willingness to follow up his victory by engaging Lee began on July 4th. Meade himself undermined his position in his congratulations to the Army of the Potomac for its work at Gettysburg. He concluded with: "Our task is not yet accomplished, and the Commanding General looks to the Army for greater efforts to drive from our soil every vestige of the presence of the invader."[17] Meade would regret his choice of words. Without knowing all the facts, Abraham Lincoln read Meade's message and with darkened face groaned: "Drive the invader from our soil? My God! Is that all?"[18] Though open to several interpretations, Lincoln's immediate reaction took Meade's words to mean that the general wanted "to get the enemy across the river again without a further collision."[19] Lincoln no longer trusted his generals, fearful that Gettysburg would be another Antietam—where George B. McClellan squandered three days following his victory. Nothing Meade said or did could diminish Lincoln's unfavorable opinion of him during this phase of the Gettysburg campaign.

Notwithstanding Lincoln's usually accurate instincts, his assessment of Meade's behavior was unfair. Contrary to the president's belief, Meade did set out after Lee for the express purpose of battling him again for, as revealed to his wife Margaret, he would rather fight "at once . . . in Maryland than to follow in Virginia."[20] Recent scholarship criticizes Meade for failure to lay pontoon bridges over the Potomac east of the concentration of forces at Williamsport or at Harpers Ferry to get south of Lee so that he could outflank the Confederates south of the river. Meade, an engineer, must have been aware of this option but obviously preferred to engage north of the Potomac.[21] This author could find no evidence or mention that Meade and his generals ever considered this flanking movement. There was also the question of whether Meade should divide his own force to perform this operation in the event the force around Harpers Ferry was inadequate for such a mission. After all, this was not Lee and Jackson at Chancellorsville where there was no river to cross following a great battle.

But the president's reaction came from trying to convince his generals that their objective should not be the possession of real estate but the destruction of Lee's army. He had forgotten all too soon that Meade's mission when appointed in June was to stop and repel Lee's invasion as well as protect Washington and Baltimore. Halleck's letter explaining Meade's mission had accompanied the order placing Meade in command. The army was to have two goals: (1) to be "the covering army of Washington as well as the army of operation against the invading forces of the rebels" and (2) it was "to maneuver and fight in such manner as to cover the capital and also Baltimore, as far as circumstances will admit. Should General Lee move upon either of these places, it is expected that you will either anticipate him or arrive with him so as to give battle."[22] Halleck told him that outside of these missions, Meade was "free to act" as he saw fit. Did Meade perform his duties well? Nowhere in the order did it say he must destroy the enemy army before it returned to Virginia (especially after engaging and defeating the army). Nor is that mission to be inferred without specific further directive. But the president believed that should the rebel army go north of the Potomac it could "never return, if well attended to."[23]

Meade's interview with Brigadier General Herman Haupt on July 5th further undermined his position. Haupt was not privy to

Meade's plan of pursuit but his interview convinced Haupt that Meade did not plan to attack Lee and he reported this view to the president, Stanton and Halleck the next day.[24] Ironically, Haupt's departure coincided with Meade's decision authorizing the army's southern march with a direct pursuit of Lee to the west by the Sixth Corps.[25] Imboden reached Williamsport on July 5th only to find the pontoon bridge destroyed by Federal cavalry and the river swollen by heavy rain making the ford impassable.

Halleck's messages from Washington came fast and furious—certainly with the prodding of the president. Halleck expressed satisfaction with Meade's movements on July 5th but his mood changed rapidly, reflecting official Washington's impatience. On July 6th Halleck wrote Meade, "You have given the enemy a stunning blow at Gettysburg. Follow it up and give him another."[26]

On July 7th, Halleck again urged an immediate attack after he received from Lincoln a message to pass on to Meade confirming the surrender of Vicksburg. This news was also intended to spur Meade on and remind him of the ideal of destroying an enemy army as Ulysses S. Grant had done. The president had forgotten that the Vicksburg campaign lasted over nine months. "Now," the president added, "if General Meade can complete his work, so gloriously prosecuted thus far, by the literal or substantial destruction of Lee's army, the rebellion will be over."[27] Meade understood the importance in destroying the enemy army. On July 5th he had written his wife, "It was a grand battle, and is in my judgment a most decided victory, though I did not annihilate or bag the Confederate Army."[28]

By July 7th Meade was convinced anyway that Lee was in retreat, gave up on direct pursuit, and ordered his army southward as he had intended to do two days earlier. His cavalry had not been passive either. Brig. Gen. John Buford's cavalry had engaged Imboden's cavalry at Williamsport and Maj. Gen. J. E. B. Stuart's cavalry turned back an assault by Judson Kilpatrick at Hagerstown. Yet despite pressure from Stuart's cavalry, Buford and Kilpatrick continued to hold their advance positions around Boonsboro until Meade could bring up the Army of the Potomac.

Using Halleck as an intermediary, Lincoln sent another message to Meade informing him that the enemy was crossing at Williamsport and that the army should move against Lee by forced marches. He emphasized that the opportunity to attack the enemy army while straddled over the Potomac should not be lost. Meade bristled and fired back a brusque reply that according to his intelligence the enemy was not crossing the river and the army was already making forced marches.[29] On July 9, Halleck backed down and told Meade not to be influenced by "any dispatch from here against your own judgment. Regard them as suggestions only. Our information here is not always correct."[30]

It is hard to imagine that this was sent with Lincoln's knowledge. Technically—if not politically and militarily—Meade could now disregard orders from Washington with impunity. And "Old Brains," as Halleck was called, actually believed, even if Lincoln did not, that, "To order a general to give battle against his own wishes and judgment is to assume the responsibility of a probable defeat. If a general is unwilling to fight, he is not likely to gain a victory."[31]

But the fury continued from Washington. Lincoln was deeply distressed and grieved over what many in the capital were already calling Lee's "escape." Such a term was highly debatable but Lincoln was sure that Meade's cautious dispatches prior to the 14th sounded too much like McClellan by pointing to his difficulties as excuses to do nothing. The president overlooked the fact that Meade had ordered an advance before he knew the Confederates had crossed the river. Yet Lincoln may also have wondered whether a reconnaissance in force feasible on the 14th wouldn't have been just as feasible on the day before.

But the president may have been unfair in his analysis. Ignorant of the topography, weather conditions, and the dynamics at work, he made it sound too simple. "We had them within our grasp," he told his secretary John Hay. "We had only to stretch forth our hands & they were ours. And nothing I could say or do could make the Army move."[32] Lincoln assumed, wrongly as it turned out, that Lee was surrounded when he uttered: "Our army held the war in the hollow of their hand & they would not close it."[33] And, at a cabinet meeting on July 17, Lincoln said that "Meade had made a terrible mistake."[34] His view was reinforced by members of the cabinet. For example, Secretary Welles complained of Meade's "want of decision and self reliance in an emergency."[35] Moreover, on July 22, 1863, Secretary of War Edwin M. Stanton wrote: "since the world began no man ever missed so great an opportunity of serving his country as was lost by his neglecting to strike his adversary."[36]

When Meade telegraphed the news of Lee's crossing the Potomac to Halleck on July 14, the general in chief replied that "the escape of Lee's army without another battle has created great dissatisfaction in the mind of the President, and it will require an energetic pursuit on your part to remove the impression that it has not been sufficiently active heretofore."[37] Clearly stung, Meade promptly telegraphed Washington and asked to be relieved of command: "Having performed my duty conscientiously and to the best of my ability, the censure of the President conveyed in your dispatch . . . is, in my judgment, so undeserved that I feel compelled most respectfully to ask to be immediately relieved from the command of this army."[38] Halleck declined the offer but the aftermath of the campaign would and continues to haunt Meade. While he remained in command of the Army of the Potomac and received a regular commission as a major general, the perception would later deprive him of the independent command he desired. Command of the Middle Military District and the troops in the Shenandoah would go to Philip Sheridan.[39]

In a letter intended to mollify Meade, President Lincoln wrote him on July 14: "I have just seen your despatch to Gen. Halleck, asking to be relieved of your command, because of supposed censure of mine. I am very—*very*—grateful to you for the magnificent success you gave the cause of the country at Gettysburg; and I am sorry now to be the author of the slightest pain to you."[40]

But Lincoln could not hide his disappointment. "Again my dear general, I do not believe you appreciate the magnitude of the misfortune involved in Lee's escape. He was within your easy grasp, and to have closed upon him would, in connection with our late successes, have ended the war. As it is the war will be prolonged indefinitely. If you could not safely attack Lee last Monday, how can you possibly do so South of the river, when you take with you very few more than two thirds of the force you then had in hand? It would be unreasonable to expect, and I do not expect you can now effect much. Your golden opportunity is gone, and I am distressed immeasurably because of it."[41]

John Hay's diary entry for July 15 notes Lincoln's depression over Meade and adds that Robert Lincoln "says the Tycoon is grieved silently but deeply about the escape of Lee. [The president] said, 'If I had gone up there, I could have whipped them myself.'"[42] While the letter was laid aside and never sent, it expresses Lincoln's most inner thoughts. Did he expect too much?

Lincoln's Prudence Resumes

Despite Lincoln's criticism, Meade had reason for not pursuing Lee more aggressively. His generals were almost all against it. They had seen the results of frontal attacks on strong positions. The rebel army had made powerful defensive positions. Lincoln was correct in seeing the strategic necessity of destroying Lee's army but momentarily he allowed this to cloud his tactical sense. He failed to comprehend the immediate realities that his officers could see only too well. His view may have been myopic—viewing the situation from the White House and the Soldiers' Home—rather than from the field.

Lincoln and Halleck shared responsibility for the troubled relationship with Meade. Lincoln was one of the few to blame Meade instead of Halleck for Lee's escape. Welles complained that: "I have been unable to see, hear, or obtain evidence of power, or will, or talent, or originality on the part of General Halleck. He has suggested nothing, decided nothing, done nothing but scold and smoke and scratch his elbows."[43]

The problem was that Halleck and Lincoln failed or refused to see what they wanted to ignore. They told Secretary Welles that he had not interfered because "Halleck knows better than I what to do . . . It is better that I, who am not a military man, should defer to him, rather than he to me."[44] The president was being disingenuous here as he was meddling in military tactics.

One should also note that Lincoln was a much better commander in chief in 1864 than in 1863. He was always learning the job. But he was asking too much from Meade, as Meade would not lose the war—even if he was not the general to win it. By 1864 with General Ulysses S. Grant in command of all field forces, Abraham Lincoln grew more patient in his battlefield expectations than he had been in 1863.

All too often Halleck failed to engineer communications between Meade and the president. Abraham Lincoln did not communicate directly with Meade because of previous problems with General Hooker.[45] All messages went through "Old Brains." But Halleck fostered bad relations between the field and Washington, telling the generals in the field that Washington was too political and did not understand the problems faced in the field[46] and then telling Stanton and Lincoln that the Army of the Potomac is no good because it did not wish to fight.[47] By 1864 Lincoln caught on and once again began talking directly to his field commander—by then Ulysses S. Grant.

To understand Lincoln after Gettysburg requires us to know who talked to the president. Such confidants put their own spin on what occurred. One of the first to talk to Lincoln after Gettysburg was General Dan Sickles, who complained of Meade in an effort to save his reputation for foolishly advancing his corps at Gettysburg and thus exposing the Federal's left flank.[48] The president also sent Vice President Hannibal Hamlin to Meade's headquarters.[49] Lincoln wanted to learn more about the situation and the reasons for Lee's crossing the river. It was a different situation from Antietam where McClellan had refused to move after the battle when he had fresh troops available. Meade did move—and he moved with troops who were exhausted.

We tend in hindsight to assume that Lincoln knew everything. But we must put ourselves in Lincoln's place. What did he actually see and who was talking to him? Lincoln received inaccurate reports from Halleck, Sickles, Hamlin, Haupt and others and these colored Lincoln's initial view of Meade and the situation. Not until he received one of Meade's corps commander's letter in defense of Meade did Lincoln come to finally comprehend what actually had occurred. General Oliver Otis Howard wrote President Lincoln on July 18, 1863, ". . . As to not attacking the enemy prior to leaving his stronghold beyond the Antietam it is by no means certain that the repulse of Gettysburg might not have been turned upon us; at any rate the Commanding General was in favor of an immediate attack but with the evident difficulties in our way the uncertainty of a success and the strong conviction of our best military minds against the risk, I must say, that I think the general acted wisely."[50] Writing to Howard, a week after Lee returned to Virginia, Lincoln perhaps finally realized his hasty and unfair conclusions after the battle. As he put it: "I am now profoundly grateful for what was done, without criticism for what was not done. Gen. Meade has my confidence as a brave and skillful officer, and a true man."[51]

As he repeatedly showed in his political roles, Abraham Lincoln grew in his role as the commander in chief. Though he often showed momentary outbursts of anger in both his political and military roles when overly frustrated, overall Abraham Lincoln is

General George Meade, astride a noble black horse, gestures toward the action as his Union troops drive Confederates from the field in the lithograph *Battle of Gettysburg, July 1-3, 1863*, by T. B. Enzel. The print was a blatant copy of the famed Gettysburg Cyclorama, which by then had likely been off public view long enough to fade into memory. By focusing on the commanding general, it suggested that Meade had been in the center of the fighting during the battle. *LC*

the epitome of the prudent leader in public office just as George Gordon Meade's performance in July 1863 was "competent, and committed to combat."[52]

NOTES

The author wishes to acknowledge the suggestions and comments of William D. Pederson and Brooks Simpson.

1. Brig. Gen. Henry J. Hunt, chief of union artillery, praised General Meade, in a letter to Alexander S. Webb, January 19, 1888, *Papers of the Military Historical Society of Massachusetts*, 14 vols. (reprint, Wilmington, 1989-90), vol. 3, p. 239; Gideon Welles, *The Diary of Gideon Welles*, ed. Howard K. Beale, 3 vols. (New York, 1960), vol. 1, pp. 374-75. Meade suffered from "want of decision and self-reliance in an emergency."

2. Gabor S. Boritt, "'Unfinished Work': Lincoln, Meade, and Gettysburg," Boritt, ed., *Lincoln's Generals* (New York, 1994), pp. 80-120.

3. A. Wilson Greene, "Meade's Pursuit of Lee From Gettysburg to Falling Waters," Gary W. Gallagher, ed., *The Third Day at Gettysburg & Beyond* (Chapel Hill, 1994), p. 163.

4. June 27, 1863, George Meade, *The Life and Letters of George Gordon Meade*, 2 vols. (New York, 1913), vol. 2, p. 3.

5. *The War of the Rebellion: A Compilation of the Official Records of the Union and Confederate Armies*, 128 vols. (Washington, 1880-1901), Series I, 27, pt. 1, pp. 173-87. All references are to Series I.

6. Meade, *Meade*, vol. 2, p. 125.

7. Ibid., p. 132.

8. *OR* 27, pt. 1, p. 91.

9. Ibid., pt. 3, pp. 532-33.

10. Ibid., pt. 1, p. 91.

11. Edwin B. Coddington, *The Gettysburg Campaign: A Study in Command* (New York, 1968), p. 569.

12. *OR* 27, pt. 1, p. 91.

13. Coddington, *The Gettysburg Campaign*, p. 567.

14. *OR* 27, pt. 1, p. 92.

15. Charles Carleton Coffin, *The Boys of '61; or, Four Years of Fighting. Personal Observation with the Army and Navy, From the First Battle of Bull Run to the Fall of Richmond* (Boston, 1885), p. 303.

16. *OR* 27, pt. 1, p. 94.

17. Meade, *Meade*, vol. 2, pp. 122-23.

18. James B. Fry in Allen Thorndike Rice, ed., *Reminiscences of Abraham Lincoln by Distinguished Men of His Time*, 6th ed. (New York, 1888), p. 402.

19. Roy P. Basler, *et al.*, eds., *The Collected Works of Abraham Lincoln*, 9 vols. (New Brunswick, N.J., 1953-55), vol. 6, p. 318.

20. Meade, *Meade*, vol. 2, p. 132.

21. Letter from Dr. Charles Zimmerman to the author, November 21, 1996. See also Chester G. Hearn, *Six Years of Hell: Harpers Ferry During the Civil War* (Baton Rouge, 1997), pp. 227-30.

22. Meade, *Meade*, vol. 2, p. 132.

23. Lincoln, *Works*, vol. 6, p. 341.

24. Herman Haupt, *Reminiscences of General Herman Haupt* (Milwaukee, 1901), pp. 223-24, 227-28.

25. Meade, *Meade*, vol. 2, pp. 130-31; *OR* 27, pt. 1, pp. 669-70; pt. 3, p. 537.

26. *OR* 27, pt. 1, p. 82.

27. Lincoln, *Works*, vol. 6, p. 319.

28. Meade, *Meade*, vol. 2, p. 125.

29. *OR* 27, pt. 1, p. 85; pt. 3, pp. 605-06.

30. Ibid., part 1, p. 88.

31. Ibid., 29, pt. 2, p. 277.

32. Tyler Dennett, ed., *Lincoln and the Civil War in the Diaries and Letters of John Hay* (New York, 1939), p. 67.

33. Ibid., p. 69.

34. Welles, *Diary*, vol. 1, p. 374.

35. Ibid., p. 375.

36. Benjamin P. Thomas and Harold M. Hyman, *Stanton: The Life and Times of Lincoln's Secretary of War* (New York, 1962), p. 275.

37. *OR* 27, pt. 1, p. 92.

38. Ibid., p. 93.

39. Meade, *Meade*, vol. 2, p. 244.

40. Lincoln, *Works*, vol. 6, p. 327.

41. Ibid., p. 328.

42. Dennett, *Diaries and Letters of John Hay*, p. 67.

43. Welles, *Diary*, vol. 1, p. 373.

44. Ibid., p. 371.

45. Lincoln has been roundly criticized for not using the chain of command and communicating through Halleck rather than communicating directly with General Joseph Hooker prior to and after the battle of Chancellorsville. With all his faults Halleck could and did act as a shield for the president.

46. Meade, *Meade*, vol. 2, pp. 138-39.

47. Stephen E. Ambrose, *Halleck: Lincoln's Chief of Staff* (Baton Rouge, 1962), p. 161.

48. Coddington, *Gettysburg Campaign*, p. 339. Lincoln visited General Sickles on July 5, 1863, at his residence in Washington where the general was recuperating from the amputation of his leg. Sickles undoubtedly repeated to the president that Meade's chief of staff had been asked by Meade to draft an order for retreat from Gettysburg. Daniel Butterfield told him that Meade had directed him to draft the order. Earl Schenck Miers, ed., *Lincoln Day by Day: A Chronology 1809-1865*, 3 vols. (Washington, 1960), vol. 3, p. 195.

49. Noah Brooks, *Washington in Lincoln's Time*, Herbert Mitgang, ed. (New York, 1958), p. 92.

50. Lincoln, *Works*, vol. 6, p. 341.

51. Ibid.

52. A. Wilson Greene, "Meade's Pursuit of Lee," p. 193.

Contributors

Richard N. Current is University Distinguished Professor of History Emeritus at the University of North Carolina at Greensboro. The recipient of the Bancroft Prize, and the Logan Hay Medal for his contributions to the Lincoln field, he has written many books and taught throughout the world.

William C. Davis is the author or editor of numerous books, including the award-winning biography of John C. Breckinridge; *Jefferson Davis: The Man and His Hour*, *"A Government of Our Own": the Making of the Confederacy*, and *The Cause Lost: Myths and Realities of the Confederacy*. Born in Kansas City, Missouri, he holds a M.A. degree in history from Sonoma State University. He spent twenty years in magazine publishing, and for many years was editor of *Civil War Times Illustrated*.

Harold Holzer is Vice President for Communications at the Metropolitan Museum of Art and a leading author on the political culture of the Civil War era. He is the author of numerous books including *Mine Eyes Have Seen the Glory:*

The Civil War in Art; *The Lincoln-Douglas Debates*; *Washington and Lincoln Portrayed: National Icons in Popular Prints*; *Dear Mr. Lincoln: Letters to the President*, and *Witness to War: The Civil War, 1861-1865*.

Edna Greene Medford is an associate professor of history at Howard University. She is the author of many articles and appeared as a commentator on the C-SPAN telecasts of the Lincoln-Douglas Debates.

Sandra Day O'Connor is an Associate Justice of the Supreme Court of the United States. She received her L.L.B. from Stanford University. A former member of the Arizona Senate, she became the first woman to hold the chief leadership position in a state legislature. Prior to her appointment to the U.S. Supreme Court by President Ronald Reagan, she served on the Arizona Court of Appeals.

William D. Pederson is the editor/co-editor of several books, including *The Rating Game in American Politics; The "Barberian" Presidency; Abraham Lincoln: Sources and Style of Leadership*, and *Abraham Lincoln Contemporary: An American Legacy*. He is a professor of political science and director of American Studies at Louisiana State University in Shreveport.

John Y. Simon is the dean of American documentary editors and has supervised the publication of the multi-volume *Papers of Ulysses S. Grant*. He serves as the Executive Director of the Ulysses S. Grant Association and professor of history at Southern Illinois University in Carbondale.

Frank J. Williams is an Associate Justice of the Supreme Court of Rhode Island. One of the nation's leading authorities on the life of Abraham Lincoln, he is the co-editor of *Abraham Lincoln: Sources and Style of Leadership,* and *Abraham Lincoln Contemporary: An American Legacy*. He serves as the chair of the annual Lincoln Forum.

On the Lincoln Forum:
An Interview With The Chairman

Frank J. Williams, Chairman of the Lincoln Forum, was asked recently to discuss the founding of the organization, and its mission as a national Lincoln association for the new millennium. He was interviewed by fellow Lincoln scholar Harold Holzer

*   *   *

HH: Why was the Lincoln Forum organized?

FW: Until the founding of the Lincoln Forum, no truly nationwide organization existed to bring together enthusiasts and scholars to explore the Civil War era and its continuing impact on the American experience. Our 1996 statement of purpose commits us "to enhance the understanding and preserve the memory of Abraham Lincoln" through such activities as the annual symposium, the semi-annual membership Bulletin, and active participation in education and preservation programs that bring together people "who share a deep interest in the life and times of Abraham Lincoln and the Civil War era."

HH: How many members currently belong to the group?

FW: After only three years, the Forum counts more than 500 members in thirty-nine states, plus Canada, sixty-five of whom are lifetime members [the full roster appears elsewhere in this volume]. The membership roster is growing quickly and we intend to continue nurturing prospects from around the country. The enthusiasm reflects the fact that the Lincoln Forum has become the national classroom for both Lincoln scholarship and Lincoln camaraderie.

HH: How important is the Forum publishing program in the organization's plans?

FW: The publication program is a crucial priority for the Forum. The current volume is but the first in what we hope will be a series of collections of the important scholarly papers delivered at our annual symposia in Gettysburg. We hope through the medium of the printed page to extend this scholarship to an even wider audience—particularly to the classroom—which hungers for serious exploration of the national past. We envision a series of "Lincoln Forum" collections on different themes.

HH: How would you characterize the Board of Advisors of the Forum?

FW: Although we retain an organizational informality, we seek counsel and ideas from our advisors at our annual meetings in Gettysburg in November, and throughout the year through correspondence and discussion. I do not think it is an exaggeration to suggest that our Board is the most prestigious in the Lincoln world. We count extraordinary scholars (Richard N. Current, James M. McPherson, Mark E. Neely, Jr., Gabor S. Boritt, David Herbert Donald, John Y. Simon, and John Keegan), major collectors (Louise Taper, Daniel Weinberg), heads of Lincoln organizations and Lincoln sites (Norman Hellmers, Michael Maione, Daniel Pearson), and major American leaders for whom Lincoln has been a particular inspiration (Mario Cuomo, Paul Simon, and Jim Edgar). Such luminaries support the Forum, its mission, and its members in countless important and inspiring ways.

HH: Does this roster change, and if so, how?

FW: First of all, each time a Lincoln organization elects a new leader, he or she automatically receives an invitation to join the Forum's Board. Thus, the new leader of the Lincoln groups of New York and Pennsylvania, for example, Joseph Garrera and Tina Grim respectively, become the newest Advisors. And sadly, we—and the Lincoln community at large—have lost two irreplaceable luminaries in recent years. The extraordinary Don E. Fehrenbacher, for example, one of the deans of Lincoln scholarship, died in 1997. And in 1998, Ralph G. Newman, bibliophile extraordinaire, died in Chicago. But the vitality of the Forum is such that we derive new strength from our new advisors, and in the past few seasons we have added Doris Kearns Goodwin, for one, whose research into the Lincoln White House will result soon in a major book and public television series.

HH: Why does the Forum meet annually in Gettysburg?

FW: Until we convened the Lincoln Forum, no national Lincoln organization met regularly in the East. Gettysburg seemed a perfect site. Its Lincoln connection, of course, is very strong. This is the village where Abraham Lincoln delivered his best-remembered public address, a testament to his faith in the Union and the rebirth of freedom, a virtual re-consecration of American democracy. And here is where thousands of soldiers who died for that cause lie buried. Lincoln would have wanted, I think, for future generations to remember the town this way. In recent years, happily, the town has heightened its focus on Lincoln, erecting a new statue outside the house in which he slept the night before the Gettysburg Address. Here the Civil War Institute thrives. And here, of course, the entire town mobilizes to celebrate the Address on its anniversary.

HH: The Forum convenes on this anniversary, does it not?

FW: The Forum meets annually in Gettysburg during the days immediately preceding the exact anniversary day, November 19. We hear our presenters and commentators and panelists, conduct our battlefield tours, hold our meetings, and stage our banquets—and then our participants are invited to the great events of Gettysburg Address anniversary day: the annual luncheon of the Lincoln Fellowship of Pennsylvania, the ceremonies and major public address at the Gettysburg Soldiers' ceremony, and the annual Fortenbaugh Lecture at Gettysburg College. The dovetailing of these events makes for an unforgettable week in what is practically the holy land of Lincoln studies.

HH: The particular highlight of the Lincoln Forum is the annual award of achievement. Can you explain how that came to be?

FW: Our Board wanted very much to create a way to honor people who have done truly extraordinary things to advance the study of and appreciation for history in general and the Civil War and Lincoln in particular—not necessarily professional historians, and never tied to a single recent achievement.

HH: Who are the Lincoln Forum award laureates?

FW: Our first award went to Professor Gabor S. Boritt, Fluhrer Professor of Civil War studies at Gettysburg College and Director of its Civil War Institute.

That was an easy choice. No one has done more in the past decade to make Gettysburg the national Mecca of serious and inviting Lincoln and Civil War scholarship. Our second award went to Brian Lamb, chairman and on-air host of the C-SPAN cable network, in recognition of what he has done to bring history alive for millions of American television viewers. C-SPAN has covered the re-staging of the Lincoln-Douglas debates in Illinois, has taken viewers on visits to Lincoln shrines across the country, interviewed leading scholars, and of course televised our own symposium. Its influence is strong and its commitment to history deep. Finally, in 1998, we honored the man many have called the historian of the century, John Hope Franklin. He had just completed his service as chairman of President Clinton's advisory panel on race relations. We wanted to express our admiration to him for bringing Lincoln's vision of equal opportunity to a century and a millennium he could not have even imagined.

HH: And the award has been newly re-named, correct?

FW: In 1998 we re-christened the award the Richard N. Current Award of Achievement of the Lincoln Forum in honor of our founding member, who is universally acknowledged as the dean of Lincoln scholars. Dick Current has been a source of knowledge and inspiration to thousands of students of the Civil War for more than 50 years, as well as an early and enthusiastic supporter of the Forum. It is truly "altogether fitting and proper," if I may borrow a phrase from Lincoln, that he be honored permanently through the award we give to honor others annually.

HH: What other activities engage the Forum's organizational attention?

FW: Education and preservation are two such issues. We are currently organizing and funding a national essay contest for college undergraduates—not just to give out prizes, which we will also do, but to engage the attention of our young people on what the past can teach them as they prepare to build the future. And we have been actively involved in a plan to preserve and restore the Anderson Cottage at the Soldiers' Home in Washington—the residence that President Lincoln and his family used as a summer retreat to escape the downtown heat. Lincoln certainly worked on his Emancipation Proclamation on this site, which qualifies it automatically as a national shrine. We have won the support of the National Trust for Historic Preservation and of First Lady Hillary Rodham Clinton, and hope to work to bring this important building back to its appearance during the 1860s.

HH: Do you support the work of other Lincoln and Civil War groups elsewhere in the country?

FW: That is an essential part of our charter. In 1996, we co-sponsored a conference on Lincoln and Emancipation in Virginia. In 1999 we co-sponsor a unique conference organized by the New York State Archives in Albany to celebrate the preservation of the state's Civil War records and artifacts, and to present scholarly papers related to New York's role in the war. It was, after all, the state that sent more troops and more money than any other for the Union cause. Yet it was also the site of the worst civil disturbances of the period—the New York City draft riots. It deserves special study.

HH: How do prospective new members join the Lincoln Forum?

FW: We continue to welcome members at all levels. They need only write to me directly at 300 Switch Road, Hope Valley, RI 02864. We can only hope that everyone who reads this book will join the Lincoln Forum, and that everyone who joins the Lincoln Forum will read this book.

The Lincoln Forum Board of Advisors

(As of April 1, 1998)

Frank J. Williams
Chairman

Harold Holzer
Vice Chairman

Charles D. Platt
Treasurer

MEMBERS

Nathanial A. Boone
Gabor S. Boritt
Roger D. Bridges
Peter G. Brown

Robert V. Bruce
Ken Burns
S. L. Carson
Joan L. Chaconas
Frank Coburn
George M. Craig
Gary Crawford
Hon. Mario M. Cuomo
Richard Nelson Current
William C. Davis
David Herbert Donald
Hon. Jim Edgar
Eric Foner
Dennis E. Frye
Gary W. Gallagher
Joseph E. Garrera
William Gienapp
Tim Good
Doris Kearns Goodwin
William Hanchett
Gayle Harris
Norman D. Hellmers
Charles M. Hubbard
John T. Hubbell
Dale Jirik
John Keegan
James P. Kushlan
David E. Long
Don McCue
Richard M. McMurry
James M. McPherson
Michael R. Maione
John F. Marszalek
Edna Greene Medford
Richard Moe
Rev. Lee C. Moorehead
Mark E. Neely, Jr.
Ralph G. Newman

Stephen B. Oates
Lloyd Ostendorf
Phillip Shaw Paludan
Paul L. Pascal
Daniel E. Pearson
William D. Pederson
Dwight Pitcaithley
Gerald J. Prokopowicz
Ronald D. Rietveld
Steven K. Rogstad
Gregory Romano
Stuart Schneider
John Y. Simon
Hon. Paul Simon
Edward Steers, Jr.
Craig L. Symonds
Louise Taper
Wayne C. Temple
Thomas R. Turner
Laurie Verge
Daniel R. Weinberg

Don E. Fehrenbacher (1920-1997)

The Lincoln Forum

Members - 1999

Mr. & Mrs. Bernard Ableman,
Wilmington, DE
Norman L. Abrams, San Anselmo, CA
Wes Achauer, Zanesville, OH
Bruce Airheart, Romeoville, IL
Gene Akers, Knoxville, TN
Jack A. P. Albertson, El Centro, CA
Edwin Allard, New York, NY
Hattie R. Allen, Washington, DC
Rev. Russell Allen, Clinton, CT
Amy Amander-Valdes, Miami, FL
Fritz Amer, Seattle, WA
Patrick N. Anderson, Alexandria, VA
Mr. & Mrs. Von W. Andrews, Ft. Collins, CO
Lana & Steven Archer, Neotsu, OR
Floyd D. Armstrong, Pensacola, FL
Steve Arnold, Decatur, IL
Greg Bailey, St. Louis, MO
Mary B. Bailey, Washington, DC
Jean H. Baker, Baltimore, MD
Garnet R. Barber, Thornhill, Ontario, Canada
Paul Barker, Toronto, Ontario, Canada
Ron & Joan Barnett, Omaha, NE
Carl Barone, W. Hempstead, NY
Ken Barton, Pompano Beach, FL
Dan Bassuk, Neshanic, NJ
James R. Baum, Providence, RI
A. C. & Delores De Benedictis,
Penn Valley, CA
B.J. Bennett, Clinton, MD
Melvyn S. Berger, Newton, MA
Richard Bernard, Burlingame, CA
Carol S. Bessette, Springfield, VA
Jill Blessman, Springfield, IL
Marceline Blevins, Weatherford, OK
Richard Books, Oklahoma City, OK
Nathanial & Harriet Boone, Manchester
Center, VT
Gabor S. Boritt, Gettysburg, PA
David Bosch, Bristol, TN
Steven L. Botney, Boynton Beach, FL
Derald Bowles, Easley, SC
Catherine Boyers, Winchester, PA
Charles G. Boyle, Long Island City, NY
Charles Brame, Alta Loma, CA

Timothy Branscum, Amherst, OH
Paul & Jaquellyn Bremer, Grand Rapids, MI
Roger D. Bridges, Fremont, OH
Carolyn Bromley, New Smyrna Beach, FL
Brophy Family, Waterbury, CT
Chris Brown, Dallas, TX
Ed & Suzanne Brown, San Antonio, TX
Karren C. Brown, Hodgenville, KY
Peter G. Brown, Dallas, TX
Robert V. Bruce, Durham, NH
Berdie Brumenschenkel, Wadsworth, OH
Mr. & Mrs. Carey Brush, Richmond, VA
Montague Buck, Washington, DC
Ken Burns, Walpole, NH
George Buss, Freeport, IL
Sally & Thomas Butler, Ft Wayne, IN
Fred & Claire Calabretta, Westerly, RI
Norman Callan, Altoona, PA
Burrus Canahan, McLean, VA
Martin & Diane Carlino, E. Patchogue, NY
Arnold Carlson, Coventry, CT
Steven L. Carson, Silver Spring, MD
Russell W. Casto III, Nitro, WV
Sam Catalino, Brandon, FL
Joan L. Chaconas, Brandywine, MD
Peggy Jo G. Chagan, West Chester, PA
Caroly & Keith Chamberlin, Ada, MI
Joe Chaney, Lakewood, CO
Newell L. Chester, Minneapolis, MN
Martin & Mary Cigledy, Falls Church, VA
Mark A. Clark, Falls Church, VA
Frank Coburn, Harrogate, TN
George Cohen, Athens, OH
Julie Hoover & Marvin Cohen, Arlington, VA
Linda B. Collins, Fountain Valley, CA
Ed & Candice Cotham, Houston, TX
George M. Craig, Elmhurst, NY
Gary Crawford, Alexandria, VA
Robert L. Cunningham, Brookline, MA
Hon. Mario M. Cuomo, New York, NY
Richard Nelson Current, South Natick, MA
Josephine Currier, Tehachapi, CA
Janice E. G. Curry, Fall River, MA
Jackie Cutlip, Bedford, TX
Eunice & Hal David, Los Angeles, CA

Brooks Davis, Chicago, IL
Bruce Davis, Camden, SC
William C. Davis, Mechanicsburg, PA
Tom Destefano, Haledon, NJ
Karen Devereux, Round Lake Beach, IL
Michael Devine, Laramie, WY
Red & June Dietz, Titusville, FL
Nicholas DiGiovanni, Wayland, MA
Jeanette E. Dixon, Silver Spring, MD
Robert Doerk, Cheyenne, WY
Stan Domosh, Delran, NJ
David Herbert Donald, Lincoln, MA
John & Cynthia Doolittle, Dexter, NY
Charlie Doty, Washington, DC
Tom H. Douglas, Amory, MS
Virginia Douglas, Centerville, OH
Roger W. Draeger, Fort Atkinson, WI
Davis G. Durham MD, Wilmington, DE
Jo Dzombak, Latrobe, PA
Alphonse D'Angelo, Franklin Square, NY
Mel Ecker, Roca Raton, FL
Hon. Jim Edgar, Springfield, IL
Carol Ellis, Glastonbury, CT
Paul F. Ellis-Graham, Highland Mills, NY
Avram Fechter, Washington, DC
Dr. Norman B. Ferris, Murfreesboro, TN
Mark A. Fields, Indianapolis, IN
Monika & Martin Fleming, Tarboro, NC
Anthony & Catherine Flynn, Wilmington, DE
Eric Foner, New York, NY
James E. Foster, Shreveport, LA
Thomas B. Fox, Brockton, MA
Steven P. Franckhouser, Berwyn, PA
John Hope Franklin, Durham, NC
Sue & William Frary, Cincinnati, OH
A. Barry Freed, Belleville, WA
Robert French, Appleton, WI
Dale G. Frye, Johnstown, PA
Dennis E. Frye, Hagerstown, MD
Gary W. Gallagher, State College, PA.
Malcom Garber, Seattle, WA
Joseph E. Garrera, Newton, NJ
Ralph Gary, Grapevine, TX
Robert Geise, Selingsgrove, PA
Arthur C. Germano, Peabody, MA
Jim Getty, Gettysburg, PA
Larry Gibson, San Antonio, TX
William Gienapp, Lincoln, MA
Marilyn Gilloon-Crotty, East Rockaway, NY
Stephen & Patricia Gilroy, E. Norwich, NY
Bill Gladstone, West Palm Beach, FL
Paul & Edith Goldman, Brooklyn, NY

Tim Good, Springfield, IL
Doris Kearns Goodwin, Concord, MA
William Gorski, Arlington Heights, IL
Paul E. Gradwell, Meriden, CT
Alfred O. Granum, Northfield, IL
Tina Grim, Gettysburg, PA
Bernard Gross, Austin, TX
Hal & Ida Gross, Flushing, NY
Michael B. Gross, Arlington, TX
Burnell R. Gulden, Lafayette, IN
Dave & Shirley Gulvin, Lincoln, RI
Lee Gunter, Naperville, IL
Kathlyn Hall, Dover, DE
Wiliam Hanchett, San Diego, CA
Chuck Hand, Paris, IL
Rev. Harold Hand, Orwigsburg, PA
George & Florence Haney, Annapolis, MD
Stanley L. Harbison, Ypsilanti, MI
Gayle Harris, Alexandria, VA
Kathryn M. Harris, Springfield, IL
Tony & Sue Harris, Somerset, NJ
William C. Harris, Raleigh, NC
James Hashman, Mount Vernon, OH
Pamela D. Hawman, Birdsboro, PA
Robert L. Heaton, Lafayette, CA
Mark N. Heidenreich, Cheektowaga, NY
C. David Hein, Frederick, MD
Norman D. Hellmers, Springfield, IL
Robert F. Henderson, Orleans, IN
Robert D. Hesterly, Fairfield, IL
Merrill & Jean Hoefer, Freeport, IL
John Hoffman, Champaign, IL
Terry & Gary Holahan, Silver Spring, MD
Fr. William Holberton, Bethlehem, PA
Jackson & Cordelia Holliday, Macon, GA
Harold & Edith Holzer, Rye, NY
John Horner, Gettysburg, PA
Robert A. Howard, Carlisle, PA
Craig Howell, Washington, DC
Charles M. Hubbard, Harrogate, TN
John T. Hubbell, Kent, OH
Richard Hughey, Aston, PA
Don & Jane Hunt, Chicago, IL
William E. Hurtig, Pembroke Pines, FL
William C. Ives, Chicago, IL
Mr. & Mrs. Elden Jackson, Sunfield, MI
Bill Jacques, Putney, VT
Richard Jamison, Downers Grove, IL
Eugene & Jane Jamrozy, Greenfield, WI
Jeffery J. Javid, Madison, WI
Laurie Jeffery, New York, NY
Bob & Jean Jenkins, Cambridge, MD

Janice Jerabek, Pleasanton, CA
Albert C. Jerman, Manchester, VT
Dale & Earlene Jirik, Topeka, KS
Bob Johnson, Chicago, IL
Gary D. Joiner, Shreveport, LA
Harry Jones Jr., Kingston, NC
Mr. & Mrs. James A. Jordan MD,
    Lauderdale by the Sea, FL
Nadine Kagan, Valley Stream, NY
Kurt M. Kausler, St. Louis, MO
Martha Kayler, Wilmette, IL
John Keegan, Warminster, Wiltshire, England
William Keisling, Lemoyne, PA
Roland A. Kelling, Wauwatosa, WI
James Kelly Family, Pembroke, MA
Richard J. Kelly, Malta, NY
Phil & Linda Kendall, Oklahoma City, OK
Donna Kerns, Winchester, VA
Kathleen Kichak, Parma, OH
Robert A. Kinsley, York, PA
Donia Kirmseé, Pasadena, CA
Bernie Kopera, Orland Park, IL
Steve Koppelmann, Randolph, NJ
Wayne E. Korsinen, Concord, CA
W. Clay Krick, Dry Fork, VA
James P. Kushlan, Harrisburg, PA
Diane M. Kushner, Wyndmoor, PA
Lisa LaBuda, Cary, IL
Michael D. Lacey, Valparaiso, IN
Everett & Antigoni Ladd, Arlington, VA
Brian Lamb, Washington, DC
Dan Laney, Austin, TX
Charles E. Lang, Lexington, KY
Robert G. Langford, Morris Township, NJ
Tom Lapsley, Fairview, OR
Robert G. Larkin, Louisville, KY
Rev. Kenneth Larter, Merchantville, NJ
William W. Layton, Millwood, VA
Naomi Lazarus, New York, NY
Rob Leete, Haslett, MI
Than Lenox, Lebanon, IN
Alan Levine, Rockford, IL
Allen & Sandra Levinsky, Binghamton, NY
Roger M. Levy, Wilmington, DE
Roy Licari, Ft Washington, MD
The Louisiana Lincolnator, Shreveport, LA
Frank Van der Linden, Bethesda, MD
Louise Lindinger, Cherry Hill, NJ
Dr. David E. Long, Greenville, NC
George P. Lordan Jr., Salem, MA
Mark & Sandra Lore, Vienna, VA
Anthony A. Loredo, Snellville, GA

Thomas P. Lowry, Woodbridge, VA
Robert Maher, Winchester, VA
Arthur C. Maimon, Durham, NC
Michael Maione, Washington, DC
Tom Mangrum, Lexington, VA
Kenneth Mangum, Phoenix, AZ
MGEN Ronald H. Markarian, Fresno, CA
John F. Marszalek, Mississippi State, MS
Cindy Martin, Bomoseen, VT
Martin Family, Southborough, MA
Richard E. Martin, Mount Joy, PA
Richard Masloski, New Windsor, NY
Kent Nickolas Mastores, Oakland, CA
Sunny Matema, Silver Springs, MD
Sandy McBride, Wichita Falls, TX
B.F. & Dorothy McClerren, Charleston, IL
Kathleen M. McCollough, Lincoln, IL
Jim McCormack, Newark, NJ
Don McCue, Redlands, CA
Jim McCullough, Rimersburg, PA
Archie McDonald, Nacogdoches, TX
Judy & Joe McKenna, Dunellen, NJ
Kevin McKenna, Flossmoor, IL
Stephen B. McKenrick, Fayetteville, PA
David & Carolyn McMorrow, Wareham, MA
Richard McMurry, Americus, GA
Jennifer McNamara, Princeton, NJ
James M. & Patricia McPherson, Princeton, NJ
Mr. & Mrs. Eugene McVicker, Gettysburg, PA
Edna Greene Medford, Bowie, MD
H. Craig Miller, Belleville, WA
John G. Miller, New York, NY
Martha Miller, Austin, TX
Richard Moe, Washington, DC
Luther C. Monk, Detroit, MI
Jeff & Sally Moore, San Jose, CA
Lee C. & Betty Moorehead, Batavia, IL
Michael Morrell, Columbia, MD
Don Morrow, Chicago, IL
Rea Mowery, San Diego, CA
Grant S. Moyer, Moorestown, NJ
Nancy & Roy Muehlberger, Scottsdale, AZ
Dale Mulligan, Crawfordsville, IN
Lee & Roselen Murphy, Oak Park, IL
Michael Musick, Harpers Ferry, WV
J. Mark Mutter, Toms River, NJ
John F. Myers, Brewster, MA
Dr. & Mrs. Nash, Westlake, OH
Mark E. Neely, Jr., University City, MO
F.D. Neilsen, Nova Scotia, Canada
Lonnie W. Neubauer, Chevy Chase, MD
Stephen B. Oates, Amherst, MA

Loyette A. Olsen, Winfield, KS
Frederick I. Olson, Wauwatosa, WI
Keith St. Onge, Edwardsville, IL
David L. Oslin, Lakewood, OH
Lloyd Ostendorf, Dayton, OH
Norris & Helen Owen, Bloomfield, IN
Dr. Patricia Ann Owens, Mt Carmel, IL
Lawrence A. O'Brien, Lothian, MD
Mark & Karen O'Connor, Medfield, MA
Jane F. O'Donnell, Gainesville, FL
Mr. & Mrs. Tom O'Neill, Ft Wayne, IN
Phillip Shaw Paludan, Princeton, NJ
T. Michael Parrish, Austin, TX
Paul L. Pascal, Washington, DC
Mary Pate, Ft Myers, FL
Robert A. Patnode, Oklahoma City, OK
Mae Patton, Los Angeles, CA
Ginny & Mort Paulson, Silver Spring, MD
Daniel E. Pearson, Beaver Dam, WI
William D. Pederson, Shreveport, LA
Joseph J. Pick, Hollywood, FL
Dwight T. Pitcaithley, Washington, DC
Allan R. Pitts, Scottsdale, AZ
Gary Planck, Winter Park, FL
Charles D. & Linda Platt, Greenwood
    Village, CO
Mark A. Plummer, Bloomington, IL
John Plumpton, Toronto, Ontario, Canada
Tim Poirier, Indialantic, FL
Jody Potts, Dallas, TX
Keith Poulter, Tollhouse, CA
Robert A. Price, Edina, MN
Dan Priest, Port Republic, ME
Polly Prokop, Jacksonville, IL
Gerald J. Prokopowicz, Fort Wayne, IN
Jim & Bonnie Quirke, Libertyvile, IL
Victoria Radford, Nashville, TN
Paul Readinger, Reading, PA
Stephen Recker, Pasadena, CA
William H. Redd, Falls Church, VA
William Reese, New York, NY
Rose & Don Reever, Addison, IL
Gene Reid, Austin, TX
Michael Bishop Rieg, Lansdale, PA
Ronald D. Rietveld, Fullerton, CA
John Roach, Staten Island, NY
William & Elaine Robin, Centerville, MA
Steven K. Rogstad, Racine, WI
Dennis Rohatyn, San Diego, CA
Greg Romano, Lawrenceville, NJ
Jeff Rombauer, Maple Valley, WA
Katharine B. Ross, Wilmington, DE

Richard Rowe, Greenville, DE
Duke Russell, Los Angeles, CA
Bob & Marolyn Rutherford, Cherry Hill, NJ
Donald A. Rydgren, Hockessin, DE
Jack Sadler, Rio Verde, AZ
Mark Sadler, Hampton Cove, AL
Gerald & Lillian Safferman, Pittsboro, NC
Barbara Sardella, York, PA
Michel Sauvage, New York, NY
Gordon & Marilyn Schafer, Holt, MI
Joseph & Catherine Schaller, Columbus, OH
Stuart Schneider, Teaneck, NJ
Philip Schoenberg, Flushing, NY
Eleanor L. Schuman, Highlands Ranch, CO
Thomas Seaver, Milford, MA
Cecelia Segurson, San Francisco, CA
Bill Seitzer, Chestertown, MD
Milton Seltzer, Wantagh, NY
Joseph Semenza, Phoenix, AZ
Dennis Sheehan, Litchfield, NH
Colleen Shogan, New Havenm, CT
Bob Siefken, Bishop, CA
Eileen Simon, Irvine, CA
Hon. Paul & Jeanne Simon, Makanda, IL
John Y. & Harriet Simon, Carbondale, IL
George Lincoln Sisson, Bristol, RI
JoAnne Six-Plesko, Madison, WI
Peter Skelly, Janesville, WI
Priscilla Sleight, Coon Rapids, MN
Henry & Miriam Slings, Spring Lake, MI
Charles A. Smith, Washington, DC
Dr. Steven A. Smith, Bridgeport, WV
Charles W. Snider, Savannah, GA
Rich Sokup, Freeport, IL
Richard Somer, Clinton, NY
John Spadea, Lemon Grove, CA
William Spears, Wichita Falls, TX
Michael Spinelli, Croton-On-Hudson, NY
Alvin Spunt, Harriman, TN
Ronald C. Stafford, Annapolis, MD
Phil Stall, Indialantic, FL
Kim L. Stam, Twain Harte, CA
Joseph M. Stanichak, Aliquippa, PA
Paul Stazesky, Newark, DE
Rev. Richard Stazesky, Wilmington, DE
Brandt N. Steele, Greencastle, IN
Edward Steers, Jr., Berkeley Springs, WV
Dr. Mark E. Steiner, Houston, TX
Patricia Stepanek, Tuuly, NY
Philip O. Stewart, Middletown, VA
Phil Stichter, Columbus, OH
Jim Stiles, Lawrence, KS

David & Clarisse Stiller, Costa Mesa, CA
Joan Lipsitz & Paul Stiller, North
    Kingstown, RI
Eleanor Stoddard, Chevy Chase, MD
Dr. Phillip Stone, Bridgewater, VA
John Storrs, Nashville, TN
Evelyn Strassberg, Cliffside Park, NJ
Michael Strassberg, Hamilton Square, NJ
James R. Stultz, Moundsville, WV
Wendy Swanson, Falls Church, VA
Mr. & Mrs. William Swayze III,
    Wilmington, DE
Joseph Sweet, Kingston, RI
Mrs. Clare Swisher, Fraser, MI
Craig L. Symonds, Annapolis, MD
Ralph Taggart, Pompano Beach, FL
Louise Taper, Beverly Hills, CA
Mr. & Mrs. Tarman, State College, PA
Janet & Madeline Tatgenhorst, Chicago, IL
Amb. & Mrs. Lawrence Taylor, Gettysburg, PA
Mary P. Taylor, Brattleboro, VT
Myles Taylor, Rockville, MD
Zach Teer, Royse City, TX
Sunderine Temple, Springfield, IL
Wayne C. Temple, Springfield, IL
Dr. Lawrence R. Tenzer, Tuckerton, NJ
James R. Thomas, Allendale, NJ
S. S. Titus, Walnut Creek, CA
Al Todres, McLean, VA
Andrew Toroney, Coatesville, PA
Tom Trafals, Geneva, IL
Hans & Rashelle Trefousse, Staten Island, NY
Mrs. Donald Trescott, Rumford, RI
Kent Tucker, Rantoul, IL
Thomas R. Turner, East Bridgewater, MA
Harold Valdes, Miami, FL
Paul Vanderveer, Drexil Hill, PA
Laurie Verge, Clinton, MD
John J. Vietas, Fall River, MA
Carl W. Volkmann, Springfield, IL
Bill Wade, Anaheim Hills, CA
Chris Wagner, Davison, MI
Dr. & Mrs. Grant Hulse Wagner,
    Wichita Falls, TX
David Walker, Van Wert, OH
Marianne Walker, Henderson, KY
Robert P. Wallace, Amawalk, NY
Robert & Anne Walters, Newtown Square, PA
Donald Ward, Prospect, KY
Jan Warner, Phoenix, AZ
Michael Wasserman, Oakland, CA
Jack Waugh, Pantego, TX

Gary Waxler, Redford, MI
Dr. Janet Weeks, Dalton, PA
Budge Weidman, W. Springfield, VA
Daniel R. Weinberg, Chicago, IL
John Welch, Boston, MA
William Welsheimer, Stuart, FL
Robert & Mary Wernle, Crawfordsville, IN
Larry J. West, New York, NY
Annette Westerby, Englewood, CO
Brad Wheeler, Hampton Cove, AL
Robert Whelan, Wilkes Barre, PA
Robert S. Willard, University Park, MD
Arthur R. Williams, Leawood, KS
Hon. Frank J. & Virginia Williams,
    Hope Valley, RI
Fred Willmer, St. Clair Shores, MI
Gordon Windle, Auburn, ME
Albert Winkler, Oren, UT
Michael Wolf, New York, NY
Elaine Wolling, Boca Raton, FL
Steven R. Wrobleski, Montgomery, IL
Irma Zelig, MD, New York, NY
Jay M. Zerin, Pomona, NY
Charles & Roslyn Zimmerman, Fair Lawn, NJ
Craig Zurlini, Aliso Viehjo, CA
Meg Zweiback, Oakland, CA

INDEX

Reader's Notes

Reader's Notes

Reader's Notes

OTHER SAVAS PUBLISHING COMPANY TITLES ON ABRAHAM LINCOLN!

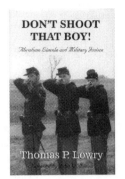

Don't Shoot That Boy!
Abraham Lincoln and Military Justice

Thomas P. Lowry

Twenty-six photos and illustrations, end notes, biblio., index, cloth, color d.j., 336pp. ISBN 1-882810-38-4. $24.95

Was President Abraham Lincoln really the compassionate soul we have been led to believe?

This thoughtful study is based on hundreds of court-martial documents in President Lincoln's own hand (most never seen or used before). Thomas P. Lowry tells each story, each life-or-death decision and the factors that tipped the balance one way or the other. Each man waited for the single stroke of the President's pen. Would it be life or death? Freedom or prison? A dishonorable discharge or a chance at personal redemption?

In the midst of America's deadliest war, Lincoln sat at the storm center of a hurricane of blood and grief, deciding the fate of men sentenced for crimes including desertion, spying, sabotage, murder, rape—the whole gamut of evil. He balanced sternness and compassion while pressed on one side by weeping relatives begging for mercy, and on the other by military leaders demanding severe discipline for an unruly citizen army. The man many have described as America's greatest president approached his thankless task with a unique blend of humor, compassion, practicality and, as Lowry describes it, "a kind of weary joy."

The 500 cases presented here, which include men of every rank, doctors, and even civilians, highlight the remarkable personalities with whom Lincoln had to deal. Union Brig. Gen. James G. Spears, for example, was a slave owner who, upon learning of the Emancipation Proclamation, exclaimed, "It is the policy of the Lincoln government to prolong the war by freeing the slaves. I say Goddamn the government; let her go to hell!!"; another general shot a sentinel dead who dared call him "an Irish son-of-a-bitch"; a colonel threw a two-day party that resulted in one-third of his regiment being AWOL and one-quarter being on sick call with venereal disease. In each of these cases, Lincoln reviewed the evidence and options of the various levels of review, and then made his final decision.

Don't Shoot That Boy! Abraham Lincoln and Military Justice is witty, fun to read, and uniquely original.

(continued)

continued from previous page. . .

What historians are saying about Lowry's new *Don't Shoot That Boy!*

"Thomas Lowry's *Don't Shoot That Boy!* confirms the notion that President Lincoln could be gentle as well as tough. These well written stories bring drama to the daily operations of war, where the President was in constant conflict between the discipline required of the military and the compassion necessary to sustain a volunteer army and navy."

Frank J. Williams, noted Lincoln scholar
and Chairman of The Lincoln Forum

"Historians who want history written from "the bottom up" might profitably emulate Dr. Thomas Lowry, who for many years has waded through court-martial records in the National Archives. In bundles of documents lie forgotten stories of Civil War misfits, soldiers who ran afoul of military justice and sometimes paid with their lives. President Abraham Lincoln's mercy is legendary. Beyond the soaring language of his Second Inaugural Address, "With malice toward none, with charity for all," lay his celebrated compassion. Lowry has discovered that Lincoln reviewed individual cases in a judicious manner, tempering the wrath of his irate officers with wisdom acquired as a prairie lawyer."

John Y. Simon, noted author
and the editor of the *Papers of Ulysses S. Grant*

A
SAVAS
PUBLISHING
FAVORITE!

Abraham Lincoln, Contemporary:
An American Legacy

Frank J. Williams
& William D. Pederson, eds.

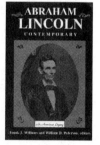

A stellar collection of articles from the first symposium on President Lincoln held in the Deep South. Includes Lincoln's impact on other presidents, his relations with the Supreme Court and Congress, his quarrelsome cabinet, and the premonitions that haunted him. Photos, biblio., notes, index, cloth. d.j., 256pp. ISBN 1-882810-01-5. $24.95.

Savas Publishing Company
202 First Street S.E., Suite 103A, Mason City, IA 50401; Voice: 515-421-7135;
E-Mail: cwbooks@mach3ww.com; Online Catalog: www.savaspublishing.com

Distributed by Stackpole Books: 1-800-732-3669